ISRAEL'S BROKEN-HEARTED PROPHET

ISRAEL'S BROKEN-HEARTED PROPHET

Hosea's Prophecy:
an Introduction and Concise Commentary

by
Malcolm C. Davis

JOHN RITCHIE LTD
CHRISTIAN PUBLICATIONS

ISBN-13: 978 1 910513 73 6

Copyright © 2017 by John Ritchie Ltd.,
40 Beansburn, Kilmarnock, Scotland

www.ritchiechristianmedia.co.uk

Typeset by John Ritchie Ltd., Kilmarnock
Printed by Bell & Bain Ltd., Glasgow

DEDICATION

*To Mr John Riddle of Cheshunt Assembly, Hertfordshire,
minister of the Word and Bible commentator, who has also
written on the Prophecy of Hosea, and
encouraged me to do the same.
May the Lord use both our books to help His people to
appreciate the truths contained in this prophecy
and to apply them to all our lives, for His glory!*

ACKNOWLEDGEMENTS

I wish to thank most sincerely the following people for contributing to the publication of this book: Mr Fraser Munro of Kennoway Assembly, Fife, for editing the manuscript and making valuable suggestions for its improvement, and also for writing the Foreword; my wife, Ruth, for continuing to encourage me in writing for the edification of the Lord's people; Mr Graham Stanley of Harehills Assembly, Leeds, for proofreading the text prior to its printing; and the staff at John Ritchie Ltd for their work of composition and printing. Without them all, the book would not have been as valuable and accurate as it now is. To God be the glory for His enabling grace to all who have become involved in its production!

Leeds, October, 2016

Foreword

At the commencement of the New Testament, a group of twelve men – the twelve disciples of the Lord Jesus. Matthew 10 verse 5 declares: 'These twelve Jesus sent forth'.

At the conclusion of the Old Testament, another group of twelve men. In some aspects, quite different from each other. Different centuries. Different classes. Different circumstances. Different countries. Yet, as Malcolm Davis points out in his Introduction, they are described collectively as 'The Twelve'. The language of Matthew 10 verse 5 can be adapted and then applied to them: 'These twelve God sent forth'. Sent forth to the people of their day – and sent forth to the people of every subsequent day, including our own.

They have acquired an unusual and rather unfortunate description: 'The Minor Prophets'. When first given, it was a reflection on the length of their writings, but the danger is that Bible students regard it as a description of their legacy. For many of us, sadly, these are neglected books. This is a tragedy.

The first of these prophets is Hosea. His is a powerful story. Hosea was a man who told a message with his lips. More than that, he was a man who told a message with his life. His wife, immoral in her character and unfaithful in her conduct. Strange that he was directed to marry such a woman – and Malcolm Davis takes the time to consider this. We see her standing in the slave market. Such is the depth to which she has descended, yet Hosea buys her back and the relationship is ultimately restored.

As Malcolm Davis very helpfully describes in this *Introduction and Concise Commentary*, the message conveyed so graphically is the relationship between the Nation and the Lord. Disobedient to the Lord and departed from the Lord, they are disciplined by the Lord – all with a view to their deliverance.

In this prophecy, we see the salvation of the Nation and they owed everything to the supreme love of God. They had been drawn 'with cords of a man, with bands of love' (Chapter 11 verse 4) and we hear the divine promise: 'I will heal their backsliding, I will love them freely' (Chapter 14 verse 4).

In their story, we can read our story. In this very old prophecy, very relevant truths for us to learn. Sinfulness leads to sorrow, but the Lord stands ready to forgive and to restore His people.

In Chapter 4, Ephraim is 'joined to idols', but as the prophecy comes to an end, Ephraim declares: 'What have I to do any more with idols? I have heard Him, and observed Him' (Chapter 14 verse 8).

Wrote the hymnwriter:

> *'Hast thou heard Him, seen Him, known Him?*
> *Is not thine a captured heart?*
> *"Chief among ten thousand" own Him,*
> *Joyful choose the better part.*
>
> > *Captivated by His beauty*
> > *Worthy tribute haste to bring;*
> > *Let His peerless worth constrain thee,*
> > *Crown Him now unrivalled King.*
>
> *Idols, once they won thee, charmed thee,*
> *Lovely things of time and sense;*
> *Gilded, thus does sin disarm thee,*
> *Honeyed lest thou turn thee thence.*

What has stripped the seeming beauty
From the idols of the earth?
Not a sense of right or duty,
But the sight of peerless worth.

Not the crushing of those idols,
With its bitter void and smart,
But the beaming of His beauty,
The unveiling of His heart.

Who extinguishes their taper,
Till they hail the rising sun,
Who discards the garb of winter,
Till the summer hath begun?

'Tis the look that melted Peter,
'Tis the face that Stephen saw;
'Tis the heart that wept with Mary,
Can alone from idols draw.

Draw and win and fill completely,
Till the cup o'erflow the brim;
What have we to do with idols,
Who have companied with Him?'

Miss Ora Rowan (1834-79)

The story told in this lovely hymn is the story told in this prophecy. Those who have benefitted from previous Commentaries by Malcolm Davis will be grateful to him for turning his attention to Hosea. He may describe it as a *Concise Commentary*, but those who read it will find it helpful and those who apply it will find it profitable. It is an honour to have been asked to write this Foreword – and a privilege to be able to commend this book to you.

Fraser A Munro
Windygates, Fife
February 2017.

Israel's Broken-hearted Prophet

Contents

Select Bibliography

In writing this commentary I have found the following books especially helpful:

Baxter, J. Sidlow. *Explore the Book, 6 vols. in 1.* Grand Rapids, Michigan: Zondervan, 1966.

Cameron, Donald C. B. *The Minor Prophets and the End Times.* Kilmarnock: John Ritchie Ltd, 2010.

Chisholm, Robert B. *Hosea* in *The Bible Knowledge Commentary: Old Testament.* Editors: John F. Walvoord and Roy B. Zuck. Victor Books, 1985.

Feinberg, Charles Lee. *The Minor Prophets.* Chicago: Moody Press, 1976.

Flanigan, J. M. *Hosea* in *What the Bible Teaches, Daniel-Micah. (Ritchie Old Testament Commentaries)* Kilmarnock: John Ritchie Ltd, 2011.

Jensen, Irving L. *Jensen's Survey of the Old Testament.* Chicago: Moody Press, 1978.

The King James Study Bible, King James Version. Nashville, Tennessee: Thomas Nelson, 1988.

MacArthur, John. *The MacArthur Bible Commentary.* Nashville, Tennessee: Thomas Nelson, 2005.

Riddle, John. *The Prophecy of Hosea* in *The Minor Prophets: their Relevance for Today*. Edited by Ivan Steeds. Precious Seed Publications, 1992.

Tatford, Fredk A. *Prophet of a Broken Home: an exposition of the Prophecy of Hosea*. Kilmarnock: John Ritchie Ltd, 2014. Republished with *Amos* and *Jonah*.

Unger, Merrill F. *Unger's Commentary on the Old Testament*. Chattanooga, Tennessee: AMG Publishers, 2002.

Introduction to the Prophecy of Hosea

1. Its Position in the Canon of Scripture

Within the canon of Scripture, Hosea's prophecy has always been ordered as the first of the twelve so-called 'Minor Prophets'. This is true in both the Hebrew and Christian canons. However, in the Hebrew canon it immediately follows, not Daniel, but Ezekiel, since Daniel is ordered with the Sacred Writings, not with the Latter Prophets. The Hebrew canon calls the Minor Prophets 'The Twelve', treating them as a unit. Their order is broadly chronological, although Joel, Amos, and Jonah may have prophesied before Hosea began his ministry. Hosea is the second longest of the Minor Prophets; second, that is, after Zechariah, which also has fourteen chapters. The Minor Prophets as a whole cover the main area of prophetic ministry in Israel from about 850 to 400 BC. It has been suggested that Hosea may have been placed first 'because of the pivotal importance of his message, being centred in God's covenant love (*hesed*), breathing the larger hope of His mercy and grace, in contrast to His dreaded justice and wrath' (M.F. Unger).

2. Its Authorship and Date

The list of four kings of Judah and one king of the Northern Kingdom of Israel in Hosea chapter 1 verse 1, namely, Uzziah, Jotham, Ahaz, Hezekiah, and Jeroboam II, son of Joash, king of Israel, proves that the prophet Hosea ministered to his people for several decades, probably for over forty years, and possibly for much longer than that. We do not know precisely when he was called by the LORD to prophesy, but it was probably towards the ends of the reigns of Uzziah and

Jeroboam II. Jeroboam II reigned from c. 793-753 BC, while Uzziah reigned from c. 790-739 BC. Hosea may have begun to prophesy c. 750 BC, or a little earlier than that. Hezekiah began to reign alone, after a period of co-regency with his father Ahaz, about 715 BC, so that Hosea's ministry probably continued until at least 710 BC, and possibly a little later than that date. His prophecy predicts the complete collapse of the Northern Kingdom of Israel to the Assyrians, which occurred in 722 BC, and, in chapter 1 verse 7, clearly promises Judah's miraculous deliverance from the besieging Assyrian army in 701 BC as a yet future event. It is likely, therefore, that Hosea's ministry ended before this actually took place. He makes no mention of the six Israelite kings who followed Jeroboam II. This fact may suggest the legitimacy of the Davidic line of kings in Judah by contrast with the instability and collapse of the kingship in the Northern Kingdom of Israel, for all these six kings of Israel came to the throne by wicked means and reigned for only short periods of time.

Attempts have been made by some scholarly unbelievers to deny that Hosea wrote parts of the book which bears his name, particularly those parts which refer to the Southern Kingdom of Judah. However, it is unnecessary to deny the Judean passages to Hosea, since, although he mainly addressed the Northern Kingdom of Israel, his message embraced the whole people of God. Other eighth-century BC prophets, such as Amos, Isaiah, and Micah, besides Hosea, addressed both kingdoms in the course of their ministries. It is suggested by some commentators that Hosea may have migrated to Judah after the fall of Samaria in 722 BC to end his days there. Also, Hosea's parallels with Deuteronomy cannot be called later additions, since Deuteronomy is correctly dated before, not after, Hosea. No, we may safely assert that the prophet Hosea wrote the whole book which bears his name.

3. Its Historical Background
2 Kings chapters 15-20 and 2 Chronicles chapters 26-32 record the events which occurred during the reigns of the

kings mentioned in chapter 1 verse 1 of this prophecy. Hosea began his ministry near the end of a period of military success and economic prosperity in both Israel and Judah. Assyrian influence in the west had declined during the first half of the eighth century, thus allowing the kingdoms of Jeroboam II and Uzziah to flourish. However, the Assyrian king Tiglath-pileser III (745-727 BC) revived their expansionist policy, and, in 733-732 BC, Israel was made a puppet kingdom within the Assyrian Empire under Hoshea, their last king. When Hoshea attempted to rebel, Israel was invaded, Samaria was besieged, the Northern Kingdom was defeated in 722 BC, and its population deported to Assyria. Judah had also become a vassal state of the Assyrian Empire under their evil, unbelieving king Ahaz, but later, under the good king Hezekiah, rebelled and was miraculously delivered from the Assyrian yoke in 701 BC. However, this probably happened after Hosea had ended his ministry.

During the days of Hosea, the Northern Kingdom of Israel was plagued by anarchy, unrest, and confusion. Seven evil kings ruled briefly in the space of about thirty years, usually coming to the throne as a result of assassination and political intrigue. Some favoured alliance with Egypt, while others favoured alliance with Assyria. The *New Bible Dictionary* explains the comments of the LORD in chapter 7 verse 11, 'Israel was like a silly dove...fluttering everywhere but to God'. Although, economically, the nation was still prosperous, morally and spiritually it was Israel's 'zero hour'. Idolatry with the cults of the Canaanite gods Baal and Ashteroth was widespread, and practised unashamedly beside the rituals of the worship of the LORD. Sexual immorality was rampant, social injustice condoned, and the majority of the people arrogantly rejected the word of the LORD through His true prophets. Israel was badly backslidden, even apostate, when Hosea preached to them, so that national disaster was imminent.

4. Its Literary and Linguistic Character

The first three chapters of Hosea's prophecy are the narrative of his unhappy marriage at the LORD's command with an unfaithful woman. The LORD gave Hosea and his wife to His people Israel as an illustration of His own unhappy contemporary relationship with them. The LORD then gave Hosea several sermons to preach to Israel on their spiritually backslidden condition, urging them to repent on pain of national disaster. In these sermons, which are written in poetry, Hosea's style is abrupt, terse, and sharp, flashing forth in brilliant sentences, some of which are difficult to interpret. With the love of God burning in his heart and tears falling from his eyes, he pleaded with his beloved people to repent and accept God's mercy and covenant love while it was still offered to them, and to change their ways. J. Sidlow Baxter has said, 'What the weeping Jeremiah was to Judah, the southern kingdom, nearly a century and a half later, that was the sob-choked Hosea to Israel, the northern kingdom'. Also, just as Jeremiah lived to see the fall of Jerusalem to the Babylonians, and the exile of Judah, so Hosea lived to see the fall of Samaria to the Assyrians, and the exile of Israel to Assyria. M.F. Unger has said that, 'with the brokenness and passion of Jeremiah, Hosea had a sensitivity of heart that made him the apostle of love, the St. John of the Old Testament'. However, an authoritarian tone pervades the book, although the usual prophetic declaration 'thus saith the LORD' occurs only four times in it. There are many symbols and metaphors throughout the book, especially those associated with marriage, but also some allusions to agricultural and rural life. Perhaps Hosea was a man of the countryside.

Finally, the reader is advised that he or she would do well to read the prophecy of Hosea in a more literal modern translation, as well as in the AV/KJV. Many verses of the book are difficult to understand in the older version due to linguistic obscurities which have been better translated in some of these more recent versions. Believing scholarship has helped to solve some of the difficulties posed by the original Hebrew Masoretic Text. However, readers should be warned that some of the smoother translations found in these more recent versions tend to hide real difficulties of interpretation which are not yet fully understood by any believing Bible scholar. In spite of this, it is true to assert that the general sense of most chapters of the book is fairly clear.

5. Its Outline

Two suggested outlines are presented here from published works with the aim of enabling readers to gain a bird's-eye view of the prophecy as a whole. The first is the one given in J. Sidlow Baxter's *Explore the Book* (1966), while the second one is Merrill F. Unger's outline in his *Commentary on the Old Testament* (2002).

J. Sidlow Baxter's Outline of Hosea
HOSEA

THE PROPHET OF PERSEVERING LOVE

PROLOGUE (i-iii) – The whole story in symbol.

<u>ISRAEL'S SIN INTOLERABLE: GOD IS HOLY (iv-vii).</u>

THE FIVEFOLD INDICTMENT (iv, v).

ISRAEL'S UNREAL 'RETURN' (vi).

HEALING MADE IMPOSSIBLE (vii).

<u>ISRAEL SHALL BE PUNISHED: GOD IS JUST (viii-x).</u>

THE TRUMPET OF JUDGEMENT (viii. 1).

These chapters throughout are expressions
of wrath to come.

<u>ISRAEL SHALL BE RESTORED: GOD IS LOVE (xi-xiv).</u>

DIVINE YEARNING (xi. 1, 4, 8, etc.).

YET ISRAEL MUST SUFFER (xii. etc.).

THE FINAL VICTORY OF LOVE (xiv).

Merrill F. Unger's Outline of Hosea

I. ISRAEL'S REJECTION AND RESTORATION ILLUSTRATED. 1.1-3. 5.

   A. Hosea's Marriage and Israel's Infidelity. 1.1-2.1.

   B. Israel's Chastening and Future Restoration. 2.2-23.

   C. Panoramic Prophecy of Israel's Future. 3.1-5.

II. ISRAEL'S JUDGMENT FOR UNFAITHFULNESS DETAILED. 4.1-13.16.

   A. Israel's Faithlessness Exposed. 4.1-19.

   B. Israel's Chastisement and Ultimate Blessing. 5.1-6.3.

   C. Israel's Disloyalty and Treachery. 6.4-11.

   D. Ephraim's Terrible Iniquity Reproved. 7.1-16.

   E. Israel's Harvest of Sin. 8.1-14.

   F. Israel's Punishment for her Sin. 9.1-17.

   G. Israel's End and the Fall of the Kingdom. 10.1-15.

   H. The Lord's Undying Love for Israel. 11.1-11.

   I. Israel's Stern Reproof for Sin. 11.12-12.14.

   J. The Penalty of Israel's Impenitence. 13.1-16.

III. ISRAEL'S BLESSING IN THE KINGDOM PROMISED. 14.1-9.

6. Its Message and Keywords

The background to the message of Hosea is the LORD's covenant agreement with Israel given to the nation through Moses in Deuteronomy chapters 28-30. There the LORD commanded His earthly people to maintain absolute loyalty to Himself alone both in their worship and in their daily conduct. Obedience to the covenant would bring them His blessing

(Deuteronomy 28. 1-14), whereas disobedience would result in judgement and eventual exile from their Promised Land. Deuteronomy 28 verses 15 to 68 list the horrifying curses for breaching the covenant. Hosea's role as a prophet was to expose and to warn Israel of the nation's serious breach of this covenant, and to announce the LORD's intention to implement the covenant curses, unless they speedily and wholeheartedly repented of their sins. However, Hosea also reaffirmed the promise in Deuteronomy chapter 30 verses 1 to 10 of Israel's ultimate restoration.

The major themes of Hosea's message can therefore be summarised in three words: sin, judgement, and salvation. Significantly, Hosea's name means 'salvation', which indicates clearly the LORD's real ultimate intention for His wayward people. In exposing Israel's sins, Hosea emphasised their idolatry. The nation had turned to worshipping Baal, the Canaanite storm and fertility god, in a vain effort to promote agricultural prosperity and human fertility through its degrading immoral practices. He compared Israel's covenant relationship to the LORD with a marriage, and accused Israel of spiritual adultery. The LORD had commanded Hosea to marry a woman who would prove to be unfaithful to him, in order to illustrate graphically His people's unfaithfulness to Himself. However, Hosea's reconciliation with his adulterous wife was intended to provide Israel with a gracious reassurance that they would ultimately be restored to their covenant relationship with their LORD God.

Hosea mentions many other sins of which Israel were guilty, including social injustice, violent crime, religious hypocrisy, political rebellion, foreign alliances, selfish arrogance, and spiritual ingratitude. Several times Hosea pleaded with his people to repent, but he did not expect a positive response, and announced imminent judgement as inevitable and inescapable. When the LORD implemented the curses of Deuteronomy chapter 28, He would inflict on them infertility, military invasion by the Assyrians, and exile to their invaders' land. Hosea emphasised the LORD's justice by affirming that this divine punishment fitted their crimes against Him perfectly.

Yet the LORD promised not to abandon Israel totally or finally, but simply to discipline their waywardness, and to turn them in a future day back to Himself, just as Hosea was eventually reconciled to his wayward wife after he had disciplined her quite severely. The whole structure of the book reflects this positive emphasis and intention. The *Bible Knowledge Commentary* lists five judgement-salvation cycles throughout the prophecy, as follows:

	Judgement	Salvation
1.	1: 2-9	1: 10-2: 1
2.	2: 2-13	2: 14-3: 5
3.	4: 1-5: 14	5: 15-6: 3
4.	6: 4-11: 7	11: 8-11
5.	11: 12-13: 16	14: 1-9

As is often stated and confirmed by the Scriptural record, judgement is the LORD's 'strange work' (Isaiah 28. 21), which He implements only when the demands of His holiness and justice require it in view of our persistent rebellion and impenitence. He really delights to bless His creatures and to enjoy close fellowship with us when we conform to His ways and character.

It will come as no surprise to us, therefore, to find that the following keywords occur quite frequently throughout the prophecy, namely:

Know (10 times); knowledge (4 times); hear (7 times); mercy (10 times); love (7 times); return (15 times); Israel (44 times); Ephraim (37 times); Judah (15 times); I will (of the LORD 57 times).

Hosea's whole prophecy breathes God's persevering love and

mercy for His backsliding people in the face of their persistent sins, and despite the necessity for disciplining them severely because of them. We are encouraged to find that the book ends with a chapter concerning Israel's future repentance and restoration.

7. Its Relevance for Today's World

There are at least three reasons why we today, whether we are already saved or still unbelievers, can benefit from reading Hosea's prophecy, as follows:

i) *Because it will lead us into a fuller appreciation of the LORD's perfectly balanced character.*

From Hosea's Prophecy we can learn that apparently opposite aspects of the LORD's character are blended together in perfect harmony in His dealings with His wayward people Israel; both His goodness and His severity, see Romans 11 verse 22. Here we learn concerning the LORD's absolute holiness, and His consequent abhorrence of all impurity such as was involved in the cultic ritual prostitution of Baal worship. Yet the book also reveals the LORD's purely-motivated love for His erring people that planned their discipline and ultimate complete restoration to fellowship with Himself. He hated the social injustice that had become so prevalent among His people in Hosea's day, as in that of His other contemporary prophet Amos. Yet He pleaded through His servant Hosea that they might repent and forsake their sinful ways, so that He could bless them again on a wholly righteous basis, although this book does not explain what that righteous basis would one day be, namely, the substitutionary sacrifice of His own beloved Son incarnate. Here the LORD is seen as a God of perfect justice, but also as a God of great longsuffering, mercy, and grace. However, the 'trysting place, where heaven's love and justice meet', which marries these two aspects of His character, namely, the cross of Calvary, is not mentioned here; that had to wait until other Scripture was written. In Hosea's day, Israel was given the graphic illustration of the prophet's tragic marriage relationship with his unfaithful wife, Gomer.

The way in which he became reconciled to her in chapter 3 is a telling portrayal of the LORD's relationship over the centuries with His earthly people Israel. Despite the fact that He is still having to discipline them for their disobedience, He is torn inwardly by a yearning love for them that will not finally forsake them, but longs to bless them fully. The LORD does not change, so He is still the same towards us today, both His redeemed New Testament people, the Church, and all those who have not yet been saved by His grace.

ii) Because what the LORD said and did to Israel in Hosea's day contains timeless lessons for all of us today, from which we are meant to learn.

Although not all Scripture is about us by a long way, this does not mean that it is irrelevant to our lives, and can safely be ignored. No, God intended us to read it in order to learn many spiritual lessons from it. 1 Corinthians chapter 10 verse 11 and Romans chapter 15 verse 4 both confirm this to Christian believers today, and unbelievers can also profit from the study of Israel's sad history in the Old Testament. 2 Timothy chapter 3 verses 14 to 17 further affirm this truth concerning the educative value of the Old Testament Scriptures especially, since Timothy would not yet have had access to many of the New Testament writings, but was exhorted to study all the Scriptures he then possessed in order to progress spiritually. Because God is unchanging and unchangeable throughout history (although His ways with men have varied somewhat in successive ages of human history), God's moral principles of dealing with mankind are basically the same in every age. Many parallels can be drawn between God's earthly people Israel and His heavenly people, the New Testament Church, so that what was true of the LORD's dealings with Israel are true of His dealings with Church believers today. Also, since a large percentage of ancient Israel were unbelievers, unbelievers today can learn lessons from the way God dealt with that nation then.

So then, what lessons can we learn from the LORD's dealings

with Israel in Hosea's day? First of all, we can learn a valuable lesson from Hosea himself. The LORD led him to enter into an unhappy marriage, in order that Hosea might share His own deepest feelings concerning His wayward people Israel, before he began to preach to them. Hence Hosea was able to preach with heartfelt passion to his people; he did not 'traffic in unfelt truth'. Are we never guilty of speaking beyond our experience? Probably not, but it had cost Hosea a great deal to speak to Israel then. What does it cost us to speak God's word? Also, do we speak the truth in love, firmly but kindly? We too often say the right thing in totally the wrong way.

Secondly, there is a lesson for all Christians today. The major charge against the LORD's people Israel was that of unfaithfulness to their covenant promises and commitments, whereas the LORD had been completely faithful to His side of the covenant. The nation had forsaken their former love for the LORD. In a similar way, the risen Lord Jesus rebukes the local church at Ephesus for forsaking their 'first love' for Him, and lapsing into mechanical orthodoxy and cold legalism, Revelation 2 verses 1 to 7. They had once been a vibrant model assembly and the recipients of a letter from the apostle Paul revealing the highest truth concerning the Church and redemption in the New Testament, but now they were in danger of having their lampstand of testimony removed, and so ceasing to exist. God demands the very first place in our spiritual affections throughout our lives as His people on pain of severe discipline. Do we always give Him this? Do we love the Lord as much now as we did when we were first saved? Hosea's prophecy challenges us to examine our hearts concerning this matter, for nothing can replace devotion to Christ.

Thirdly, both the LORD's people and the unconverted can learn from Hosea's ministry that God has an unalterable moral law that what we all sow, that we reap, often in this life as well as later in eternity, whether this is good or bad. Israel had 'sown the wind' by their idolatrous and immoral behaviour, and therefore it followed that they were about to 'reap the whirlwind', chapter 8 verse 7. 'God is not mocked', whoever we think we are, Galatians 6 verse 7. We must not deceive ourselves about this solemn truth. Therefore, let us sow to the Spirit, not to the flesh, and so reap eternal life, not corruption. Let all readers be warned!

Fourthly, and related to this third point, we learn from this prophecy by Hosea, as we do from other parts of Scripture, such as Isaiah, Jeremiah, Ezekiel, and Habakkuk, that often the LORD uses heathen nations to discipline and judge both His own people and the unsaved. The Assyrians were the rod of the LORD's anger, see Isaiah chapter 10 verse 5. The LORD would one day send the Babylonians, 'that bitter and hasty nation' (Habakkuk 1. 6), to take disobedient Judah into their exile later, although the heathen nations were actually worse morally than the LORD's people. The arrogant Babylonian monarch Nebuchadnezzar was raised up to be the LORD's servant in chastising many other heathen nations, see Jeremiah 25 verse 9.

Finally, we find here too that the LORD is always a God of recovery and salvation to those who repent and forsake their evil ways. Throughout the prophecy, passages of judgement are relieved and balanced by passages predicting the LORD's gracious future ways in salvation and restoration. God has by no means finished with His ancient earthly people Israel, and will restore and deliver a faithful remnant of the nation at Christ's second coming in glory to reign in His Millennial Kingdom. Romans chapters 9-11 confirm this in the New Testament. Yes, Israel has a future, praise the LORD! Therefore, God will never forsake us, His parallel heavenly people, in spite of our waywardness and persecutions, for that is the clear implication of the chapters in Romans about Israel. 'The gifts and calling of God are without repentance', Romans 11 verse 29. Be encouraged, fearful saints today!

iii) Because it is evident from present world conditions that the world is now approaching another predicted time of judgement, the Tribulation and the Second Coming of Christ in glory to reign.

Just as the Northern Kingdom of Israel was facing judgement and exile at the hands of the Assyrians in Hosea's day, so unbelievers today are facing an even more cataclysmic series of judgements for their sins and rejection of Christ in the impending Tribulation, which is predicted in many Scriptures in both Testaments, and notably spelt out in detail in Revelation chapters 6-19. Many features of the world scene in our present day clearly resemble the features which will pertain at the beginning of the seal judgements predicted in Revelation chapter 6. Israel has been back in their land in unbelief for quite a long time, surrounded by hostile Arab and other nations. The present power-blocks in the political world resemble those envisaged in the prophecies concerning events during the end times. Through vastly improved technology, the world has become a global village. Moral conditions have deteriorated sadly since the Second World War, so that the days of Noah and Lot are being repeated, as the Lord Jesus said they would immediately before His Second Coming. Ecumenicalism is widespread, paving the way for the rise of Babylon the Great after the Lord has raptured His true Church to heaven. During the past two hundred years the modern missionary movement has grown dramatically and has reached most areas of the world. Also during that time, there has been a development of interest among true Christians in prophetic studies greater and better informed than ever previously in the Church Age. In fact, Scripture prophecy has begun to be fulfilled before our very eyes, although it is not yet clear exactly how everything will work out.

All this means two things for us today. First of all, it means that all unbelievers in Christ and His gospel of grace should be warned seriously to flee from the wrath of God in the coming Tribulation by repenting of their sins and trusting in Christ for salvation before it is too late to escape its judgements. The author of this book earnestly warns his unbelieving readers to wake up to their danger, to repent, and to embrace God's offer of salvation from their sins in Christ, who loves them and died for them, but will one day be their Judge, if they refuse to trust Him now as their Saviour in this life.

However, secondly, and more happily for all Christians living today, it means that we should lift up our heads in eager anticipation of our final redemption, since Christ's coming for the Church is imminent, and could easily occur during our lifetimes. The Rapture will have no necessary preceding signs; it could happen at any moment. Yet we should not be surprised that we are seeing in our days the foreshadowings of events which Scripture indicates will happen shortly after we have been translated to heavenly glory with Christ. In the light of all these things, true believers should be encouraged by the certain hope of seeing Christ very soon and of being at home with Him forever. Maranatha, our Lord is coming! Praise His name!

Hosea's prophecy also ends on a very joyful note in chapter 14 with the prospect of Israel's certain final salvation and restoration. The LORD's programme for Israel is somewhat different from that for the New Testament Church, but both Israel and we Church believers will, along with all Old Testament saints and the Tribulation saints, together enjoy the blessings abounding in Christ's Millennial kingdom on earth, which the Old Testament prophet Hosea clearly predicted and anticipated himself. Sin and Satan will not have the last word in this world's sad history. The LORD and His Christ will do so. Hallelujah!

Concise Commentary on Every Chapter

CHAPTER 1

The LORD's call to Hosea to enter an unhappy marriage relationship which would illustrate His own unhappy covenant relationship with His unfaithful people Israel

1. The circumstances and duration of Hosea's prophetic ministry, verse 1.

Hosea's name means 'salvation', and is the same as that of Hoshea, Israel's last king in Samaria. Joshua was also originally called Hoshea (AV Oshea), see Numbers 13 verses 8 and 16. Nothing is known of Hosea's father, Beeri, which means 'a well', nor do we know into which tribe of Israel he was born. Hosea ministered as a prophet during the reigns of four kings of Judah, of whom three were relatively good, but one, Ahaz, was very bad. He must have begun to prophesy to the Northern Kingdom of Israel near the end of Jeroboam II's reign, and would have lived through the short reigns of his six evil successors, until the Assyrians conquered Israel in 722 BC. Thereafter, he may have migrated into Judah, and must have ended his days during the reign of good king Hezekiah. See the Introduction for further details of his period of ministry, which lasted for the greater part of the second half of the eighth century BC. Although Hosea prophesied mainly to the Northern Kingdom of Israel during its last few decades, he did include the Southern Kingdom of Judah within the scope of his prophecies.

2. Hosea's call by the LORD to marry a woman who would prove adulterous as an illustration of Israel's unfaithfulness to Himself, verses 2-3a.

Chapters 1-3 contain the narrative of Hosea's unhappy

marriage, at the LORD's express command, to a woman whom He predicted would prove adulterous. The LORD's purpose in so instructing His faithful servant was to portray by this means His people Israel's unfaithfulness to their covenant relationship with Himself. Thus Hosea, through the heartbreak of his own marriage tragedy, came to see Israel's sin against their God in its deepest and most awful significance, namely, that it had hurt God and must be justly punished by Him. These first three chapters therefore set the tone of the whole series of sermons which the LORD gave Hosea to preach to His wayward people.

Other prophets, such as Isaiah and Ezekiel, were also sometimes given commands by the LORD to do things which are surprising, and perhaps, to our minds, somewhat questionable. In Isaiah chapter 20 verses 1 to 20, Isaiah was told to go naked and barefoot for three years as a sign to his hearers. In Ezekiel chapters 4 to 5 verse 4, Ezekiel was told to enact some unpleasant signs to instruct his hearers concerning their sins and the LORD's punishment for them. Here, some commentators have suggested that Hosea's marriage was only visionary or allegorical, not literal, in order to avoid the supposed moral difficulty of a holy God commanding His servant to marry a woman of bad character. However, the narrative is straightforward, and contains none of the features of apocalyptic visions. Others take the more likely view that Hosea's wife, Gomer, was sexually pure at the time of their marriage, but later became an adulteress. Certainly, Hosea appears not to have inherited a family upon marrying Gomer. Thus, probably, the LORD was deliberately anticipating what Gomer would later prove to be: an adulterous wife who bore children who were the result of her adultery. Hosea thus knew from the outset of his relationship with Gomer what would happen later. We wonder whether Gomer knew of the words of the LORD to Hosea before they came together? At all events, if Gomer was pure before she married Hosea, this situation would perfectly illustrate the LORD's relationship with Israel, who had at first been faithful to their covenant God, but later lapsed into idolatry and all manner of sins. The 'children of unfaithfulness' were thus not born as a result of sexual activity before marriage, but as a result of wrong relationships after marriage.

The second half of verse 2 proves that Hosea's marriage was to become an illustration to his people Israel that they had committed great unfaithfulness against their LORD God, and had apostatised from Him. Hosea obediently went and took as his wife Gomer, the daughter of Diblaim. Perhaps, at the time of their union, there was no sign of what was to happen later, but Hosea must have been very apprehensive of what the LORD had told him would soon happen to him. His was a hard pathway as the servant of his LORD, but he must have acknowledged the sovereignty of his God in his life. Have we? Are God's purposes and glory at the centre of our lives, or do we really only live to please ourselves? God's way is sometimes the hardest way possible.

3. The birth of Jezreel to Hosea, and the meaning of his name explained, verses 3b-5.

Verse 3b states that Gomer first bore Hosea a son. This implies that the child was born of a pure relationship between Hosea and Gomer, not as a result of any illicit union on Gomer's part. However, the LORD told Hosea to name his son 'Jezreel', which means 'God sows', as a reminder that God would soon judge the house of Jehu for the blood he shed in Jezreel, when the kingdom was taken from Ahab and Jezebel, and God's judgement was inflicted on them, see 2 Kings 9. At this point in the chapter, the significance of the boy's name was not in its meaning, but in its association with past and future events at the place called Jezreel. Jezreel was the place where Jehu had ruthlessly massacred the house of Ahab, and would also be the site of Israel's military defeat by the Assyrians. Although Jehu had killed Joram, Ahaziah king of Judah, 42 of Ahaziah's relatives, and many priests of the Baal cult in broad accordance with the LORD's will, as commanded by Elisha, he had acted in hypocritical zeal, and had not subsequently followed the LORD, but had still worshipped the idolatrous calf images set up by Jeroboam the son of Nebat. We today must consider how pure our motives are in implementing the commands of God in Scripture. Disaster will follow if we fail to apply the truth in love and grace.

Jeroboam II, king of Israel, was the fourth king in Jehu's dynasty. Hosea's prophecy against Jehu's dynasty was fulfilled in 752 BC, when Shallum assassinated Zachariah, who was the last of Jehu's descendants to rule the Northern Kingdom of Israel, see 2 Kings 15 verse 10. Hosea also here predicted the final end of the Northern Kingdom after their defeat by the Assyrians in the valley of Jezreel, the Plain of Esdraelon, which has been the scene of many famous battles throughout history and will be again. He later witnessed the fulfilment of his own prophecy, see chapter 10 verse 14. This occurred between 734 and 722 BC.

4. The birth of Lo-Ruhamah, and the significance of her name, verses 6-7.

In verse 6, Hosea states that Gomer conceived again, and bore a daughter. He does not say that Gomer bore 'him', that is, Hosea, a daughter, probably implying that Gomer had been unfaithful to Hosea, and had conceived by another man. The LORD told Hosea to name the child 'Lo-Ruhamah', which means 'Not Pitied', or 'No Mercy', explaining that this was a sign that He would no longer have mercy on Israel, so that He should at all forgive them for their sins. Israel's iniquity was now full, and the LORD must punish them with exile. Let us not presume on God's grace and longsuffering forever, but confess our sins immediately we become conscious of them. Then we will find mercy and forgiveness.

Verse 7, however, is most encouraging. Here the LORD promises that He will have mercy on the house and kingdom of Judah, at least in the near future, probably because they had not yet reached the depths of sin in the Northern Kingdom, and had enjoyed the reigns of several godly kings of the house of David. In fact, Judah continued as an independent kingdom for another century and a half, until 586 BC. This would not be due to any military might of theirs, but solely due to the direct and supernatural help and intervention of the LORD their God. The most conspicuous occasion when the LORD saved Judah from certain defeat by the besieging Assyrian army was in 701 BC during Hezekiah's godly reign, when, at a critical moment, an angel of the LORD destroyed 185,000 Assyrian soldiers in one night, and caused Sennacherib to retire from the siege of Jerusalem in abject humiliation, see 2 Kings 19 verses 32 to 36 and Isaiah 37 verses 35 to 38. Hosea's prediction primarily refers to this unique occasion, when the LORD demonstrated that He could save His people, if their ways conformed to His covenantal requirements. Sadly, after that, later kings of Judah forsook the LORD and made the Babylonian exile inevitable, despite a brief revival under godly king Josiah. However, this verse proves that obedience to God is always the right policy and sure to gain His blessing, whereas disobedience is disastrous both in this life and in the next.

5. The birth of Lo-Ammi, and the significance of his name, verses 8-9.

After Gomer had weaned Lo-Ruhamah, which in those times might have taken a few years, she conceived again, and bore another son. However, Hosea again does not say that she bore him a son, which probably implies that the boy was conceived as a result of another illicit relationship on Gomer's part. Hosea must have been terribly distressed about the situation in his family, but God said that he should name the boy 'Lo-Ammi', which means 'Not My People', to signify the sad fact that He was at least temporarily breaking off His relationship with Israel because of their sins against Him. However, this was to be only a temporary situation, as is proved by the next two verses, several other passages later in Hosea's prophecy, and many other Scriptures in both Testaments. The original unconditional covenant promises made by the LORD to the patriarchs still stand, and can never be broken. Israel must be severely disciplined, but will never be finally cast off. Only the unbelieving apostates in the nation will perish eternally.

6. The first prediction of Israel's future restoration, verses 10-11 and chapter 2 verse 1.

Immediately juxtaposed to the LORD's declaration that He is rejecting His people Israel is this encouraging promise of their certain future restoration and prosperity. As Paul asserted in Romans chapters 9-11, Israel will not be cast off forever, but will be saved as a nation in a future faithful remnant at Christ's Second Coming in glory. Many times this theme appears throughout the Old Testament prophets. Hosea's prophecy is no exception to this truth. His declarations of judgement are always balanced by predictions and promises of salvation and restoration. We should note here that, in the Hebrew Bible, chapter 2 begins at our chapter 1 verse 10, a more logical chapter division than that found in our English translations.

In verse 10, the LORD promises that, despite the imminent demise of the Northern Kingdom, in a future day the Israelites would again become as numerous as the sand on the seashore, in fulfilment of His unconditional promise to Abraham, see Genesis 22 verse 17 and Genesis 32 verse 12. In the same place where Israel was called 'Not My People' (Lo-Ammi) they will be called 'the sons of the living God', who by His almighty power and grace can accomplish such miracles. This implies that they will be born again and enjoy full fellowship with their covenant LORD God again. These verses are quoted by Paul in Romans chapter 9 verses 25 and 26 to prove that vessels of mercy would one day be found among the Gentiles. Here in Hosea the LORD is affirming that Israel will be restored to receive His blessing. Both things are true, although Paul's quotation of these verses is an application of them, rather than their primary interpretation. Yes, Israel will be reinstated.

Then, in verse 11, the LORD promises that, at the time of Israel's restoration, namely, the beginning of the Millennial Kingdom, the two kingdoms of Judah and Israel, which had been divided ever since Rehoboam's time in 931 BC, will be regathered and reunited under one head, or Leader, namely, the ideal future Davidic King of the Millennial Age. Compare chapter 3 verse 5, where this is made explicit. This is a Messianic prophecy of Christ as 'great David's greater Son'. In 2 Samuel chapter 7 verses 11 to 16, the LORD had promised David an everlasting house, or dynasty, and this covenant will be fulfilled in the future rule of Christ. It is not clear what role the Old Testament David will have in resurrection, although he may have one, perhaps as Christ's vice-regent in the kingdom. Ezekiel also predicts a mortal prince of Judah who will have important duties in the administration of Christ's kingdom, see Ezekiel chapters 44-46.

Verse 11b predicts that the united nation will at that time come up out of 'the land', possibly meaning Egypt, that is, a second Exodus, out of the land of the Gentiles, where they have been scattered for many centuries since the first century AD. The great 'day of Jezreel' referred to at the end of the chapter, is a play on the meaning of the name of Hosea's first son, Jezreel, which literally means 'God sows'. It alludes to the time when the LORD will sow, or plant, His chosen earthly people Israel in their Promised Land. It is likely that it also bears its geographical and historical significance as the place where Gideon gained a great military victory over the Midianites, see Judges chapter 7. Thus, instead of reminding Israel of their humiliating defeat there by the Assyrians in Hosea's day, it will remind them of their greatest-ever triumph in the future through Christ at the campaign of Armageddon just before the inauguration of His worldwide kingdom.

Thus chapter 2 verse 1 sums up the glorious hope of Israel's future restoration to their LORD God. The restored nation was then to say to their brothers and sisters, their fellow-Israelites, that the LORD's relationship with their nation had been re-established. Instead of calling them 'Not My People', Lo-Ammi, and 'Not Pitied', Lo-Ruhamah, as in Hosea's sad day, they were to be called once again 'My People', Ammi, and 'Pitied', or 'Mercy', Ruhamah. Then the LORD's prediction through Moses in Deuteronomy chapters 28-30 would be completely fulfilled. Paul also foresaw this time of Israel's restoration through the believing remnant at Christ's Second Coming in Romans chapter 11 verses 25 to 32. No, the New Testament Church has not replaced Israel in God's purposes of grace. We believers today are simply God's heavenly people parallel with God's earthly people Israel, but with a heavenly, not an earthly, hope and destiny.

CHAPTER 2

The LORD's prediction of His punishment of Israel for their sins, but then His promise that He will ultimately restore them in the Millennial Kingdom

The remainder of chapter 2 largely reiterates the truths stated in chapter 1, all based on Hosea's unhappy marriage relationship with Gomer, which is intended to illustrate, clearly and graphically, the LORD's unhappy covenant relationship with His people Israel.

1. The LORD solemnly warns Israel that He will punish them for their sins, verses 2-5.

Here the LORD speaks as the aggrieved Husband, and accuses Israel as His adulterous wife. He told the few faithful Israelites in the Northern Kingdom, of whom the LORD once told Elijah there were seven thousand (1 Kings 19. 18), to plead His cause against their nation's spiritual prostitution. 'Plead' has here the thought of 'contend with', or 'bring charges against', Israel for their sins. He urges the nation to put away their sins, which probably included ritual prostitution as part of the worship of the idolatrous Baal cults, because these were breaking His relationship with them as their spiritual Husband.

He warns them that, if they do not do so, He will strip them naked, like an adulteress prior to her summary execution, and deprive them of their natural fertility, for immoral ways can lead to infertility. Nor would He have mercy on her children, because they had been conceived as a result of adulterous relationships. The LORD's people Israel had acted shamefully, and had even expressed their intention to continue to pursue their idolatrous lovers, because they mistakenly believed that they, not the LORD, were the source of all their food and possessions. Sadly, how blind sinners are to the truth, and determined to persist in their sinful ways!

2. The LORD declares how He will punish His unfaithful people Israel, verses 6-13.

Now the LORD announces just how He would punish His people like an adulterous wife. He would block all means of access to these lovers with thorns and stone walls. When Israel realised that they could not find these illicit lovers any more, they would decide to return to their first Husband, on the ground that they had been better off with Him than they were now, but this would not be evidence of true repentance. Because they still thought that it had not been the LORD, but the Baals, who had supplied all their needs of corn, wine, and oil, the LORD would sovereignly deprive the nation of their agricultural produce, and leave them destitute. Leviticus chapter 26 verses 3 to 13 and Deuteronomy chapter 28 verses 1 to 14 had warned Israel that agricultural prosperity would depend entirely on their faithfulness to the Mosaic covenant. Disobedience would bring drought, pestilence, war, death, and exile upon them, see Leviticus 26 verses 14 to 39 and Deuteronomy 28 verses 15 to 68. Thus the LORD was announcing that He was about to implement His covenant curses on Israel. He would treat them like a disgraced wife without mercy. The coming judgement would cause all Israel's joyful feasts to cease, and destroy all her vines and fig trees, because His apostate people mistakenly imagined that they had received these blessings as a result of worshipping idols, not the LORD. He would severely punish them for all the time that they had worshipped the Baals and had forgotten Him, their true God. Their forgetting had been a deliberate and determined rejection of Himself, who had alone redeemed them from Egypt and blessed them in their Promised Land. Even believers today are warned by the apostle John to guard themselves from idols of all kinds, which displace God and Christ from the throne of our hearts, see 1 John 5 verse 21. The danger is evidently still with us. Be warned!

3. The LORD promises that, after He has disciplined Israel in this way, He will restore them to Himself again as His wife, verses 14-23.

Verse 7 had suggested that the LORD's dealings with Israel will eventually bring them to a state of despair, in which they would again look to Him for help. We know from other Scriptures, such as Zechariah chapter 12, that this will not finally happen before the end of the Tribulation and the coming of Christ in glory to deliver them from their enemies. Not before that moment, when, after they have suffered terribly at the hands of the Beast, they 'will look upon Me whom they have pierced', will the whole nation deeply repent of their sins against the LORD and decisively turn back to Him again. Hosea does not spell all this out in any detail, but simply speaks of the LORD courting Israel again in the wilderness with tender loving words of comfort. The LORD will restore His covenant relationship with His ancient people Israel under new conditions in Christ's Millennial Kingdom, see Ezekiel 36 and Jeremiah 31. Israel will again be called the wife of the LORD, see Isaiah 62.

When the LORD leads Israel out of the wilderness, where He has disciplined them during many centuries of the Dispersion, into their Promised Land again, He will restore their vineyards to their former productivity, and even make the valley of Achor, which reminded them of Achan's serious sin at Jericho, into a door of hope, not of judgement and punishment any more. There they will sing the song of redemption as they did when they first came up out of Egypt, see Exodus 15. In that

Millennial day they will call the LORD 'my Husband'; they will not call Baal their master. In fact, the LORD will stop Israel from speaking about the Baals at all, or remembering them. Idolatry will then be finally eradicated from Israel. Verse 18 predicts that Israel's return to their Promised Land will bring lasting peace. The Lord will mediate a covenant between the nation and the animal kingdom, so that they become tame and herbivorous. This states what Isaiah chapters 11 and 65 predict in greater detail. Also, warfare will be abolished, and there will be universal peace, see Isaiah 2 and Micah 4 for the same prediction. Then Israel will be united with their LORD forever on a righteous basis and enjoy His lovingkindness and mercy. Both the LORD and Israel will be faithful to one another, and Israel will know, or acknowledge, the LORD experientially, because His Holy Spirit will have regenerated, and have come to indwell, them, see Ezekiel 36 and Jeremiah 31.

In verses 21 and 22, the promise of verse 15 concerning agricultural blessing is expanded upon. Different elements in the natural world are personified as calling out to one another to produce fertility, and the LORD Himself joins in the chorus. This will all add to the agricultural prosperity of the earth, so that the meaning of the name of Hosea's first son, Jezreel, or 'God sows', will be fulfilled. Verse 23 expands on this thought again in connection with the LORD's relationship with Israel His people. We should note that, in its primary interpretation, it only concerns Israel and their ultimate restoration to covenant relationship with the LORD. It pictures the LORD Himself engaging in agricultural work. In the coming Millennial Age, He will plant, or sow, Israel in the Promised Land, where they will grow under His kindly protective care. Whereas in Hosea's day the nation was called Lo-Ruhamah, or 'Not pitied' or 'Not loved', and Lo-Ammi, or 'Not My people', then the nation will find mercy and love with the LORD, and be owned by Him as His people once again. Israel will call the LORD, not the Baals, 'my God'. These verses are parallel with chapter 1 verse 10 and chapter 2 verse 1, where the same reversal in the significance of Hosea's family's names is found.

This is the primary interpretation of these passages in Hosea chapters 1-2. However, Hosea chapter 2 verse 23 and chapter 1 verse 10 are quoted twice in the New Testament, in Romans chapter 9 verses 25 and 26 and in 1 Peter chapter 2 verse 10. Paul in Romans chapter 9 quoted both passages in Hosea to prove that both Jews and Gentiles will become 'vessels of mercy', that is, will be converted during the present Church Age. Likewise, Peter, in his first letter chapter 2 verse 10, applied Hosea chapter 2 verse 23 to Gentile believers today. This does *not* mean that these apostles equated Gentile believers in the Church Age with Israel, so that the present New Testament Church has replaced God's ancient people Israel in God's purposes. No, for Paul, in Romans chapter 11, also clearly predicted that national Israel would be saved as well, after 'the fullness of the Gentiles' has come in, that is, after the Church Age is over and its largely Gentile believers have been taken to heaven. Rather, Paul and Peter were *applying* to the Gentiles in the Church Age a principle concerning God's dealings with mankind in grace. It is an *application* of the passages in Hosea, *not their primary interpretation* at all. New Testament believers from the Gentiles as well as the Jews have been brought by divine mercy into an even closer relationship with God as His heavenly people, which is parallel, but not identical, with God's ancient earthly people Israel. This has been called 'the law of double reference' in understanding Scripture. In their primary interpretation, the passages in Hosea only referred to Israel, but the New Testament writers have applied a principle in them to Church believers today, Jew and Gentile. Thus this passage does not support Replacement Theology, which holds that, since the Jews rejected Christ at His first coming, God has replaced Israel in His purposes of grace by the New Testament Church, so that earthly Israel has no future at all, and the Church has taken over all Israel's promises of blessing in only a spiritualised way. No, Israel has a future, immediately traumatic, but ultimately glorious in Christ's Millennial Kingdom. We Church believers today can learn parallel spiritual lessons from the

LORD's dealings with Israel in the Old Testament, but have a somewhat different and heavenly calling, destiny, and hope from those of earthly Israel, see Romans 15 verse 4 and 1 Corinthians 10 verse 11.

CHAPTER 3

The LORD instructs Hosea to become reconciled with his adulterous wife Gomer, in order to illustrate His own future restoration of His people Israel to His favour and blessing in the Millennial Kingdom of Christ

1. Hosea's costly reconciliation with Gomer, verses 1-3.
It costs a faithful believer a great deal to make the initial effort to become reconciled with someone they love, but who has proved unfaithful and hurtful to them in a very personal way. Yet that is exactly what the LORD instructed Hosea to do to Gomer, in order to illustrate graphically His own deep love for His wayward and idolatrous people Israel. The LORD spoke somewhat obliquely to Hosea about Gomer, in view of their sad estrangement. Hosea still loved Gomer, although she had proved to be an adulteress. In the same way, the LORD still loved the children of Israel, in spite of the fact that they had put their faith in other gods, and had come to love the raisin cakes which were offered to them in idolatrous rituals. Note that the 'flagons of wine' mentioned in the AV/KJV translation are more correctly idolatrous raisin cakes eaten by the worshippers. This is one of several places in the book where our older translation is somewhat inaccurate, and therefore requires correction by a more recent translation, such as the RV, JND, and all more literal recent versions.

Pure human love is more a matter of the will to act in love than many today suppose, not just a superficial and carnal emotion, which may last for only a short time. If anyone had reason to renounce his wife for her behaviour towards him, Hosea had, but the LORD told him to express genuine love to Gomer again, in order to achieve a reconciliation with her.

Accordingly, Hosea paid a price to redeem his wife which was indicative of the depths to which Gomer had sunk in immorality. Fifteen pieces of silver was just half the price of a slave in Israel, see Exodus 21 verse 32. Barley was considered to be food fit only for animals to feed on, so one and a half homers of barley is calculated to be just ten bushels of animal food. Immorality always degrades and debases its slaves. Hosea then told his errant wife to wait for him for many days, devoting her life to him alone, and not engaging in prostitution again, nor having any lovers at all, even himself, her rightful husband, as a measure of strict discipline. The Hebrew phrase in verse 3 'thou shalt not be for another man' means literally, 'nor shall you have a man' at all. The last phrase may mean that Hosea was going to abstain from sexual relations with Gomer for many days. Gomer's time of immorality was finally over. This reminds us of Deuteronomy chapter 21 verse 13, which explains the procedure to be followed with a woman taken captive in war, but whom her Israelite master wanted to marry. For a month she was to remain in his house, but was to be separate from him, lamenting her captivity, and only after that could she become his wife.

2. The LORD predicts Israel's present time of discipline, followed by their repentance and restoration in the latter days, verses 4-5.

Hosea's tragic experience with Gomer was all a poignant illustration of how the LORD would discipline, but finally redeem and become reconciled with, His idolatrous people Israel. First, in verse 4, He spoke of Israel's present time of separation, deprivation, and discipline. Ever since their exiles to Assyria and Babylon, and even more so since their Dispersion to all parts of the world following their rejection of Christ at His first coming in humiliation, the nation of Israel has been without several things from which they had benefitted previously. Hosea had particularly in mind in this passage the government and worship of the Northern Kingdom, since both of these had been established in rebellion against the Davidic dynasty ruling in the Southern Kingdom of Judah, and the divinely appointed place and manner of sacrifice there. This explains why he includes reference to images, an ephod, and teraphim, all of which were associated with idolatrous worship and divination to seek guidance. However, Judah later became similar to the Northern Kingdom of Israel, which means that this verse is now equally applicable to Israelites who originated from the Southern Kingdom.

The present age is a time of divine discipline for all Israel, while the New Testament Church is being called out from all nations to be the Bride of Christ. Israel have actually been without three kinds of things for all this time. First, they have been without a monarchy of any sort since 586 BC, when Nebuchadnezzar removed Zedekiah from his kingship in Judah. They have had neither a king, nor a prince. Secondly, they have been without a sacrificial system ever since the destruction of the Second Temple in AD 70. Thirdly, they have certainly been without any idolatry since the destruction of Solomon's Temple in 586 BC. The exiles and the Dispersion have cured the LORD's earthly people of that previously persistent sin with all its trappings, such as images, ephods, and teraphim.

However, verse 5 predicts what will be Israel's response to this prolonged period of discipline in the latter days, that is, in the Messianic Age, from the beginning of Christ's Millennial Kingdom. God's 'afterwards', that is, His blessings after a time of hard discipline, are always well worth waiting for and experiencing. At the end of the future time of 'Jacob's trouble' (Jeremiah 30. 7), that is, the Great Tribulation, when the nation of Israel sees who it is who is coming to save them out of it, namely, the Messiah they crucified, they will repent nationally with great mourning, and seek the LORD their God and David their king, see Zechariah 12. This reference to 'David their king' may simply be a way of describing Christ, the Son of David, as 'great David's greater Son', the Branch from the root of Jesse, who will restore the spiritual life and fortunes of the Davidic dynasty in the Millennial Kingdom, see Isaiah 11. Or it may include the Old Testament king David in resurrection glory as Christ's vice-regent in the kingdom. This is not completely clear in the relevant Scriptures which predict David in the coming kingdom. There will also be a mortal, believing prince of Judah who will have some important administrative responsibilities in the reign of Christ, according to Ezekiel chapters 44-46. The fulfilment will explain everything perfectly. Repentant Israel will fear the LORD then, that is, come trembling to Him, and acknowledge His goodness in the blessings of the New Covenant which He will make with them, see Jeremiah 31. All this will be fulfilled 'in the latter days', which cannot now be too far in the future from our own times. Yes, Israel has a glorious future with their LORD God, after they have repented of all their sins and present unbelief. Praise the LORD for the glory of His grace!

CHAPTER 4

The LORD through Hosea indicts Israel for their many sins against Him

The remainder of Hosea's prophecy consists of sermons which the prophet preached to his people Israel. They expand on the message of the first three chapters, which were so graphically illustrated by Hosea's unhappy marriage to Gomer. Gomer is not mentioned again in the book, but the LORD's people Israel now take centre stage as His unfaithful wife. Although the major emphasis of the sermons is on Israel's sin and their imminent punishment in the Assyrian exile, all three major sections of the book (chapter 4 verse 1 to chapter 6 verse 3; chapter 6 verse 4 to chapter 11 verse 11 and chapter 11 verse 12 to chapter 14 verse 9) end on a positive note by predicting Israel's ultimate repentance and restoration to the LORD.

1. The LORD's case against Israel is introduced, verses 1-3.

In this chapter the guilt of the Northern Kingdom of Israel is Hosea's main theme. It mainly contains many valid accusations, but there are also hints in it of coming judgement. Hosea's sermon, or speech, takes the form of a lawsuit, because Israel had been held accountable to their LORD God ever since they had agreed to keep the terms of the Mosaic covenant, see Exodus 19 verses 7 and 8.

In verse 1, the LORD accuses Israel, because there was no truth (or faithfulness), mercy (or lovingkindness), nor knowledge of Himself throughout the land, which should have been an example of these qualities of character to all other nations. Instead, there was only swearing, lying, murder, stealing, and adultery. There was rampant and habitual bloodshed, even at government level, for Jeroboam II was succeeded by six other kings in quick succession, most of whom came to the throne by violent means, and died in the same way. Thus there was no personal or public security. Therefore, the whole country, both its inhabitants and its animals, birds, and fish, would suffer from the effects of a severe drought brought upon them providentially by the LORD as a punishment for breaking their covenant promise to Him; see Deuteronomy 11 verses 11 to 17.

2. The guilt of the priests is highlighted, verses 4-11.

In verse 4, the LORD charges the whole population alike with guilt. This meant that none of them should enter lawsuits against one another, nor oppose His charges, because all of them alike were guilty of rebellion against His law. They were like people who shamelessly defy God's established legal authorities, such as the priests, and therefore they deserved to be punished. Verse 5 probably announces their downfall, and the fall of their prophets, either by day or by night. Their mother, that is, the Northern Kingdom of Israel which supported them, would be destroyed by the LORD. Here we should remember the sad fact that both the priests and most of the prophets in that breakaway kingdom had been appointed, not by the LORD's commandment, but by the kings of the rebellious kingdom from the time of Jeroboam the son of Nebat soon after the division of the kingdom in 931 BC. They were thus a corrupt and counterfeit priesthood and school of prophets, not recognised by the LORD.

However, in verse 6, the LORD holds these leaders in the nation to account for their people's lack of knowledge of Himself and His law, because they professed, however falsely, to represent Him to their people. God judges men and women on the ground of their profession, regardless of its reality. The LORD would reject these priests, because they had forgotten the true law of their God, and He would also forget their children, that is, He would ignore their children, meaning probably that they would not inherit their fathers' office, so that the priestly line would have no future.

Verse 7 states that, although the number of these priests had increased, it had brought no benefit to the moral climate in the nation, but only further sin. They had evidently gloried in their sins, so the LORD purposed to turn their false glory into shame by judging them. Verse 8 accuses them of feeding on the people's sins by encouraging the latter to offer more hypocritical sacrifices, from which they were entitled to receive portions. Thus they set their hearts on iniquity, not on promoting holy living at all. Both the people and the priests in the nation would be punished by the LORD for their evil conduct. Despite their greed in accumulating food, their appetites would not be satisfied, because the coming drought would make food scarce. Also, their efforts to promote fertility through the ritual prostitution of the Baal cults would not succeed; they would have no children. All this was the result of ceasing to obey the LORD and breaking the terms of His covenant, the result of engaging in prostitution and drunkenness, which undermine and destroy all spiritual life and appreciation.

3. The guilt of the people is explained, verses 12-19.

It was incredible that the LORD's chosen people, with access to His wisdom, should engage in pagan worship practices with inanimate idols and seek guidance from them by divination with a pagan wand. Their immoral cultic practices had caused them to go astray from the LORD their God. They were sacrificing to heathen idols on mountain tops, and burning incense to foreign gods under every kind of convenient tree. This was accompanied by ritual prostitution with pagan priestesses, probably associated with the Canaanite Baal cults. The women who engaged in this immoral behaviour would not be singled out for punishment alone, however, since the men-folk frequented the idolatrous shrines as well to commit adultery with them. Yet the end result of this behaviour would be that the whole nation, because it was without understanding of true divine wisdom, would come to ruin.

In verse 15, the LORD through Hosea warns Judah not to imitate her sister-kingdom of Israel in their pursuit of ritual prostitution as a way of worship. Let them not begin to visit the well-known cultic pagan sites in the Northern Kingdom, such as Gilgal and Beth-Aven, which in better days spiritually had been associated with the true worship of the LORD. Beth-Aven, which means 'house of iniquity', is the way Hosea referred to Bethel, 'the house of God', where Jeroboam the son of Nebat had set up an idolatrous calf-image to replace the worship of the LORD in the temple at Jerusalem. They were not even to have the audacity to say with an oath there, 'The LORD lives', since this would be the worst hypocrisy.

Verse 16 says that, because Israel refused to repent, they had separated themselves from the LORD's protective care, like a stubborn heifer, not like a tender responsive lamb which is allowed to graze in open country. Because the Northern Kingdom of Israel, which is here called Ephraim, the name of its largest tribe, was so strongly attached to its idols, the LORD was going to leave them alone to suffer the results of their folly. Their very daily drink was rebellion, ritual prostitution was their continual practice, and their rulers, who should have protected their people from such things like shields, loved only shameful deeds. The first line of verse 19 means, literally, 'the wind has enveloped her with its wings', meaning that, as a consequence of this despicable behaviour, the whole nation would soon be swept away into exile in Assyria. Then all their idolatrous sacrifices would prove to be only a source of disappointment and shame to them.

This chapter causes the present writer to reflect seriously on the sadly immoral conditions prevailing in many countries of the world today under the guise of the permissive society, and to consider with apprehension where it is leading us. The idols of today's society may have different names and forms, but they have much in common with those of the Canaanite Baal and Asherah cults of the ancient world. Today sexual licence is encouraged as if it were healthy and normal. Drunkenness is not really frowned upon, but thought to be a legitimate form of pleasure. Truthfulness is not always encouraged, if it is thought not to be politically correct. Kindness towards our neighbours is not always practised, if it does not benefit ourselves also. Many consider that there are no moral absolutes, but that everything is morally relative to particular situations. Most people do not like to retain the knowledge of God in their thinking, and, at best, treat Him like a convenient insurance policy. They love their idols in the business or entertainment worlds rather than their Creator, and will believe the unproved claims of atheism instead of the Scriptures. Self is at the centre of their lives, not the God who sent His Son to save them. This is all leading to the dreadful conditions which the Scriptures indicate will prevail just prior to the Second Coming of Christ, 'the days of Noah', and 'the days of Lot'. Those days led directly to cataclysmic judgements by God on this world, and so will these. Reader, be warned!

CHAPTER 5

The LORD announces that He will punish Israel for their sinful rebellion

In this chapter, although the Northern Kingdom of Israel remains Hosea's main focus of his sermon, Judah, which had been warned not to follow Israel's bad example, is brought within the scope of the LORD's judgement.

1. The LORD reiterates Israel's guilt and says that it is punishable, verses 1-7.

The LORD addresses the whole nation of Israelites, but singles out the priests and the royal household for particular condemnation, since they had been in a position to exercise justice in the nation, but, instead, had encouraged the false worship at the cultic sites of Baal and Asherah, which had been such a snare to their subjects. Mount Tabor was in northern Israel, while Mizpah was either the town in Gilead, or the town in Benjamite territory, in the south. Either way, the idea is that false worship had permeated the whole country. The rebellious priesthood was deeply involved in slaughter, despite the fact that the LORD had repeatedly rebuked them for these sins. In His omniscience and omnipresence, the LORD knew all about Ephraim's wicked immorality; they could not hide it from Him. The whole land of Israel was defiled. Their lifestyle would not allow them to turn in repentance to their God; the very spirit of prostitution was rampant among them, and they had not come to know the LORD in salvation. The nation's proud arrogance served as a legal witness against them concerning their guilt, and was leading them to experience the truth of the well-known proverb, that pride goes before destruction, and a haughty spirit before a fall, Proverbs 16 verse 18.

Sadly, the LORD knew that Judah would fall into the same sins and suffer the same downfall as their sister-kingdom in the north. Although the idolaters would go with abundant flocks and herds to seek the LORD's favour by offering insincere sacrifices, they would find no forgiveness, because the LORD would withdraw Himself from them and not respond to them. Because they had been unfaithful to their covenant relationship with Him in their adulterous worship, and had begotten pagan children as a result of their ritual prostitution, the false religious festivals, such as the New Moon, would actually hasten their punishment, and not avoid it at all. Their allotted portions of land would also be destroyed by invading armies and various pestilences.

2. The LORD announces that both Israel and Judah would be destroyed by invading armies, verses 8-14.

The LORD warned His people that soon the cities of Benjamin in the south of the country, Gibeah, Ramah, and Beth-Aven (or Bethel), would be on military alert, resounding to the sound of the ram's horn and trumpet alarms. Let Benjamin beware! In the day that the LORD rebuked His people for their sins, Ephraim, the strongest tribe among them, would be helpless and defenceless. The LORD's predictions had always been accurate and would certainly be fulfilled. Even Judah would not ultimately be spared from invasion, because their leaders had offended against the LORD's commandments, such as the theft of their neighbours' boundary stones. The LORD would pour out His wrath on them like a flood of water. Hosea foresaw that Ephraim would be oppressed and completely crushed by their enemies, because they had wilfully lived according to the vanity of humanly devised principles. The Septuagint and the Syriac translation here seem to read a word which means 'vanity', that is, futile idols or ideas, instead of the AV/ KJV translation 'after the commandment', which is difficult to understand in the context. The NASB translates verse 11b thus, 'because he was determined to follow *man's* command', where the word *man's* is added to make the meaning clear. This may be correct in context. Therefore, the LORD says, He would be like a moth to Ephraim, eating away at the moral fibre of the nation, because of their inner corruption, and like corrosion to Judah for similar reasons. The two kingdoms recognised their deteriorating condition, but, instead of turning in repentance to the LORD, they resorted to political expedients in order to attempt to solve their problems. Israel formed a political alliance with the Assyrians, first under their king Menahem, and later under their last king, Hoshea. Under the evil unbelieving king Ahaz, Judah had also formed a political alliance with the king of Assyria, who is here called 'King Jareb', or 'King Contention', which may be a nickname for Tiglath-pileser III, in order to win his help against Syria and Israel. Neither alliance solved any of their problems, but led their nations into further corruption and idolatry, and simply encouraged the Assyrians to invade them. In fact, the LORD used these Assyrian monarchs to tear the two kingdoms to pieces like two lions as a punishment for their lack of faith in Himself.

At first, Judah was saved from the Assyrians by the LORD's direct intervention in 701 BC, because godly king Hezekiah fully trusted Him (see chapter 1 verse 7), but later, under several ungodly kings, even the Southern Kingdom was destroyed by the Babylonian monarch, Nebuchadnezzar, in 605, 597, and 586 BC. Both kingdoms went into exile: Israel into Assyria in 722 BC; Judah into Babylonia between 605 and 586 BC. These exiles were the LORD's sovereign actions, so that no one could rescue His apostate people from their enemies' savagery.

3. The LORD decides to withdraw from Israel until they express repentance for their sins, verse 15.

Like a lion which has torn its prey apart, the LORD says that He will retreat into His lair, and will ignore His people's prayers and cries for help, until, in desperation for the renewal of His covenant relationship, they confess their grave sin against His holiness and seek His face of favour again. Withdrawal of fellowship and blessing by God is a severe discipline, but it has the gracious object of encouraging His people's restoration. He predicts here that, in their severe affliction, His people will diligently seek His face in confession and sincere prayer. This will ultimately happen at the appearing of Christ to deliver Israel from their enemies, after they have suffered greatly in the Tribulation judgements and persecutions, see Zechariah 12-14.

CHAPTER 6

The LORD's reply to Israel's expression of repentance outlining their guilt again

The chapter division here is unfortunate, since the first three verses of chapter 6 are closely linked with the last verse of the previous chapter, which explains the way in which the LORD is acting towards His erring people, in order to secure their complete repentance. There are thus two sections in chapter 6.

1. Israel's expression of repentance, which is at first insincere, verses 1-3.

Commentators are somewhat divided on the question of the sincerity of this expression of repentance. Some rightly point out that the later verses in the chapter, which lament the transient covenant faithfulness of both Israel and Judah, strongly suggest that, certainly at the time when Hosea preached these words, the LORD's people were not sincere in their repentance at all, but very hypocritical. Others suggest that here we are meant to hear the words of Hosea himself representing the small faithful remnant of believers in his day pleading on behalf of their nation, or that the words anticipate the very true repentance of the whole nation in a day yet future to us, when Christ appears to them, as previously mentioned. Perhaps we can benefit from both thoughts, and are not obliged to accept just one view or the other.

Certainly, in Hosea's day, neither Israel nor Judah were truly repentant for their wickedness, on account of which the LORD had torn them like a fierce lion by means of the Assyrian invasions. They presumed, wrongly, that their restoration to blessing was an easy matter, and required no brokenness of heart on their part for their persistent sins. Until we feel the gravity and horror of our sins in the sight of a holy God, He cannot even begin to restore and heal us.

Verse 2 may mean that they imagined that the LORD would restore them very quickly, in a matter of just two or three days, a very short time. It is unclear what the two days followed by the third day represent. Interesting suggestions have been made, including an allusion to the resurrection of Christ, who is the true Israel, and the possibility that the two days represent two thousand years of Israel's exile and Dispersion, followed by their future restoration in the third thousand years. History may confirm this possibility, since it is over 2700 years since Israel went into exile, and their restoration in the end times is probably not far away from our own times. However, the first view mentioned above, that they mean just a very short time, is a distinct probability in the context. No, restoration from backsliding is neither easy nor cheaply obtained; it requires much heart-searching, self-judgement, and humility before it is fully accomplished. Our sins hurt God, and He had to sacrifice His only beloved Son in order to prepare the way for our forgiveness and cleansing. Forgiveness is not mechanical, automatic, or formal, but dependent upon our deeply sincere confession, repentance, and forsaking of our sins. Israel will not be ready for this before the Second Coming of Christ. Then He will shower upon His chosen people the blessings of the New Covenant like the refreshing latter and former rains in the Promised Land, and they will go on to know the LORD in daily experience as never before.

2. Israel and Judah's sadly unrepentant condition exposed, and judgement announced, verses 4-11.

In these verses, the LORD through Hosea laments the sad fact that He does not know how to produce repentance in His wayward people, including both Israel and Judah; so perverse are they. Their professed covenant love to Himself, expressed in their ritual sacrifices and offerings, is as transient and short-lived as a morning fog or the early dew. He had hewed them in pieces by means of the messages of His true prophets, in an attempt to bring His people to their senses, but all to no avail. His judgements (sent to chastise them) had been as plain to understand as daylight, but they had not responded positively to them. He did not want their ritual sacrifices at all, unless they were the expression of true practical covenant mercy, love, and faithfulness. He wanted them to know Him experientially and to live in accordance with His character, not to continue offering hypocritical worship. However, like the first man Adam and all his fallen descendents, they had continually broken His covenant with them by flagrant transgression. They had been as unfaithful to Him, as Gomer had been to Hosea.

Verses 8-10 contain lurid examples of Israel's treachery. Gilead in the north-east of the Northern Kingdom is singled out as a place where sinners practised gross iniquity, so that it is defiled with much blood. Bands of robbers there ambushed unwary travellers. Even the groups of priests on the way to Shechem were murdering people, and committing infamously sinful acts. The LORD had had to witness horrible crimes being committed in the kingdom of Israel. There was spiritual adultery in Israel, probably including ritual prostitution with the Canaanite Baal cults, and this was defiling them as the LORD's chosen earthly people. No, Israel was not then ready to repent and to be restored to the LORD's blessing, not by a long way.

Verse 11 should probably be divided into two halves. The first half should be linked with the previous verses. The LORD is probably warning the Southern Kingdom of Judah that they also had a harvest of judgement coming to them in due time because of their particular sins. Although they had the Davidic dynasty and the Temple worship, they had begun to commit sins as bad as those committed by the Northern Kingdom of Israel. However, their punishment would not come before the Babylonian monarch, Nebuchadnezzar, invaded their territory later in 605-586 BC, over a century later. The second half of the verse should probably be linked with chapter 7 verse 1; the chapter division here also is unfortunate.

CHAPTER 7

The LORD through Hosea reproves Israel's terrible sin and failure to repent

1. Israel's sin is too great to ignore, since it has reached even the king's court, verses 1-7.

If we attach the second half of chapter 6 verse 11 to the beginning of chapter 7 verse 1, then the first half of the latter verse can be translated meaningfully in this way: 'Whenever I wanted to restore the fortunes of My people (chapter 6 verse 11b), whenever I wanted to heal Israel, the sins of Ephraim are exposed and the crimes of Samaria are revealed'. In other words, Israel's stubborn rebellion and sinfulness frustrated the LORD's fervent desire to bless and restore His wayward people to Himself. He found that He must, reluctantly, punish them instead. Ephraim was the royal tribe of the Northern Kingdom of Israel, and Samaria was their royal capital city, but even there sin flourished. They were committing fraud and theft, while bands of robbers were plundering people's possessions in the countryside around. To make their sin worse, they took no account of the fact that the LORD was remembering all their wicked deeds with a view to severely punishing them before long. He saw and knew all about their deeds. In fact, they were surrounded by them like enemies, for habitual sinning brings on its perpetrators its own retribution. Their sins also affronted His holiness, so that He could not ignore them.

Verses 3 to 7 speak of the corruption and wickedness of the royal court and even of the king himself. Israel's rulers were, sadly, no different from their subject citizens. In fact, the royal courtiers entertained the king with their accounts of their wicked deeds, immoral stories, and corrupt jokes. They delighted the royal princes with their lies. All of them were adulterers, probably both spiritually and morally. Their unbridled lust is likened to a baker's oven, which is heated so hot that the baker did not need to stir up the fire from the time the dough was kneaded and had risen, until it was ready to be baked. Consider here also the fact that leavened dough is in Scripture likened to sin, which corrupts everything it is allowed to affect. The baker mentioned here is like the courtiers, who, between 752 and 732 BC, assassinated four of Israel's kings. It is this political intrigue that is the background for verses 5-7. There is here outlined by Hosea a description of how the conspirators carried out their murderous plots. On the day of the festival of their king, possibly the anniversary of his enthronement or perhaps his birthday, his princes and courtiers made him drunk with wine, so that in his unguarded moments he partied with his mockers, who were really only bent on mischief. They were actually waiting for an opportunity to kill him. Their murderous intent was like an oven which is smouldering secretly all night ready to break out into a blaze in the morning of their planned crime. In their passion for power they were as hot as an oven, and had succeeded in destroying their rulers. All their kings had fallen by their hands, most of them assassinated in palace revolutions. Sadly, none of Israel's citizens looked in true faith to the LORD, who alone could ensure the kingdom's stability.

2. *The senseless folly of Israel's rulers in forming foreign alliances to ensure the nation's political security, verses 8-12.*

Instead of turning to the LORD in faith for help, Israel's rulers had initiated a futile foreign policy of alliances with heathen Gentile nations in a vain attempt to gain political security. The LORD had intended His people Israel to remain separate from all other nations and to trust in Him alone for protection, but they had deliberately disobeyed His will in this matter.

From Solomon's time onwards, foreign alliances had always led Israel to adopt the idolatrous and immoral ways of their heathen neighbours; that was why the LORD had been so insistent on demanding their complete separation from all other nations. However, their king Menahem had paid tribute to the Assyrian king Tiglath-pileser III to buy his help. One of his successors, Pekah, had joined a coalition against Assyria, which Tiglath-pileser easily crushed. Then their last king, Hoshea, after accepting Assyrian domination for a while, stopped paying them tribute and made an alliance with Egypt. This led directly to the Assyrian invasion of 722 BC, and to the collapse and exile of the Northern Kingdom.

Therefore, in verse 8, the LORD likens Ephraim, the Northern Kingdom, to a cake not turned over in baking. They had mixed, that is, compromised, themselves with the surrounding heathen nations and adopted their wrong ways. They had, like the cake, been burned on one side by the Assyrians, but remained uncooked on the other side. They were therefore useless to the LORD, and He would soon discard them in the exile. In verse 9, the LORD through Hosea uses another simile for Israel, namely, an elderly man who has failed to notice the gradual effects of his ageing process, in particular his greying hair. This is evidence of the result of his compromise with foreign nations, who have gradually drained Israel's strength by demanding regular payments of tribute money, and thus removed their political autonomy.

Yet, verse 10 says, Israel were too proud to acknowledge their sins and foolishness to the LORD, nor were they at all prepared to return to Him in repentance or to seek to follow Him, their covenant LORD God. Israel was like a silly, senseless dove, fluttering everywhere but to their God. Sometimes they allied themselves with Egypt, at other times with Assyria, neither of whom were their true friends. Therefore the LORD said that, when they sent delegations to these countries with a view to securing their help, He would spread His net over them to capture them like a fowler catching a bird in a trap, and would chastise them with the punishments about which their congregations had heard their true prophets warning them so frequently.

3. The LORD laments the unrepentant condition of His people Israel which deserved His punishment, verses 13-16.

In verse 13, the LORD through Hosea pronounces a woe of destruction upon His unfaithful people for running away so far from Him and for transgressing so flagrantly against Him. He was sad, because it had been He who had originally redeemed them from Egypt, and yet they had been speaking lies against Him, impugning His holy and gracious character. They wanted a good crop of corn and a plentiful harvest of grapes for new wine, and had wailed and cut themselves like pagans on their beds at night when the crops failed, yet they had not cried to the LORD their covenant God in repentant and believing prayer for these blessings as they should have, but had rebelled against Him. The LORD had been particularly grieved with them, because it had been He who had trained and nourished them to full strength so that they could serve Him. Yet they had only devised evil against Him; they had shown Him no gratitude at all for His gracious ways with them. They had returned to seek help in their times of distress, yet not to the LORD, the Most High God, but to the Canaanite Baal cults. They were like a faulty bow, which is unreliable because it has been made wrongly. Despite the skill of the archer using it, it shoots its arrows wide of the mark. As a deserved punishment for their rebellion and insolent words spoken in their anger against the LORD their God, their leaders would fall in battle by the sword of their invading enemies, and would become an object of derision among the Egyptians, whose help they had so foolishly sought in their foreign alliances.

CHAPTER 8

The LORD instructs Hosea to announce Israel's punishment of invasion and exile for forsaking Him in favour of other gods and foreign nations

This chapter highlights several specific aspects of Israel's rebellious attitude towards the LORD, and announces God's imminent judgement for it.

1. Israel is especially condemned for their idolatry, verses 1-7.

For the second time in the book, the LORD orders Hosea to put the ram's horn trumpet to his mouth, in order to sound the war alarm to His people Israel, because the Assyrians were about to invade the Northern Kingdom like a swooping eagle bent on seizing its prey and carrying it off; compare chapter 5 verse 8 for the first mention of the trumpet alarm. The invasion was in fulfilment of the covenant curse on Israel for breaking their promise to keep the Mosaic Law. Deuteronomy 28 verse 49 predicts such an invasion by a foreign power for Israel's disobedience, even though He says that they are 'the house of the LORD', His own redeemed household, or family. Here the LORD specifically states that it will happen, because Israel have transgressed His covenant and rebelled against His Law. In their desperation at the time of the invasion, Israel will cry out to the LORD, claiming that He is their God, and that they know Him, but they will speak in hypocritical pretence, not sincerely. Their prayers in that crisis will not be answered, because in their daily lives they had rejected what was good. So the LORD would allow their enemies to pursue them out of their land. They had totally ignored the LORD their God when they had appointed their successive kings; they had not consulted Him, but had resorted to political assassinations. They had done likewise with their other leaders. Rather, they had instead made idols for themselves out of silver and gold, and had worshipped them. This would result in Israel being rejected at least temporarily as the LORD's people.

In particular, in verse 5, Hosea mentions the molten calf-image of Samaria, because it epitomised the idolatry of the Northern Kingdom. This image had actually been set up in Bethel and Dan since the time of Jeroboam the son of Nebat, not in Samaria, the capital city, but Samaria here represented the whole of the kingdom. The LORD said that He rejected this object of worship, and that it had aroused His anger against them. He asked plaintively how long His people would be incapable of purity in their worship of Him. The calf-idol had originated from Israel, not from Him in any way. A human workman had made it, so it was not God at all. Therefore, the LORD declared that it would be broken in pieces as utterly futile. Israel had sown a terrible crop of sin, and would now reap the whirlwind, that is, terrible retribution for what they had done. Hosea continues his agricultural metaphor when he says that Israel's annual crop would be worthless, just stalks without grain, and if they did manage to produce anything, even that would be swallowed up and taken away by foreign invaders, so that they could not benefit from it. This, again, was a fulfilment of the covenant curses of Deuteronomy 28, inflicted because of their disobedience.

2. Israel is to be swallowed up in the Assyrian Exile for their foreign alliances and idolatry, verses 8-14.

Israel was already being swallowed up and destroyed by their foreign policy, especially their alliances with Assyria. The Gentiles would not respect them at all for these, but treat them like a worthless broken vessel which cannot be a pleasure to anyone. Their king Menahem had made an alliance with Assyria for protection like a prostitute hiring lovers. Israel had been behaving like a wild ass, acting in stubborn independence and burning with sexual desire for a partner. However, despite Israel's attempt to protect themselves by forming alliances with the surrounding Gentile nations, the LORD would bring them back from their wanderings to Egypt and Assyria in order to refine them in His smelting-pot. They would begin to diminish through their sufferings for a little while as a result of the burden imposed on them by 'the king of princes', that is, the king of Assyria, Tiglath-pileser III, who had exacted a huge sum of tribute money from Menahem, see 2 Kings 15 verses 19 and 20.

Israel was also condemned for their rampant idolatry. Because they had built many altars for the purpose of conducting idolatrous rituals, which always involved committing gross sin, the LORD would allow them to become addicted to sinning in this way, in order that they might then reap the disastrous consequences of so doing. His people had ignored the many plain commandments of the Mosaic Law which He had given them, thinking that they were a strange, alien, and irrelevant thing to them. They thought that they knew better than that, as many sinful people do today when they are told of the principles of Biblical morality and the true worship of God. As for the sacrificial gifts which Israel were still offering to Him in hypocritical worship, the LORD took no delight in these offerings, because His people did not seek His glory in offering them, but were merely seeking to satisfy their own carnal desires in eating them. Therefore, the LORD did not accept them, nor did He ignore their iniquity, but determined to punish their sins by sending them into exile. When, in verse 13b, the LORD says that Israel will return to Egypt, He probably means that they will return to slavery like their bondage in the land of Egypt, although not actually in Egypt this time, but in Assyria. The context clearly indicates this. Egypt is a symbol for the place of future exile and bondage, and is so used in Hosea in several other references within his sermons; see chapter 9 verses 3 and 6, and chapter 11 verses 5 and 11.

Verse 14 highlights Israel's sad apostasy from the LORD their Maker; they had forgotten all that He had done for them, and were building themselves magnificent palaces instead. Judah were little better, for they were multiplying fortified cities in order to defend themselves, instead of trusting the LORD to defend them. However, the LORD would send a fire to destroy those cities and their citadels. This prophecy was fulfilled in 701 BC, when the later Assyrian king Sennacherib invaded Judah and destroyed all their fortified cities apart from Jerusalem itself, which he besieged and threatened to capture also, see 2 Kings 18 verse 13 and Isaiah 36 verse 1. On that occasion, because Hezekiah turned to the LORD to seek His help in his extremity, the LORD supernaturally delivered Jerusalem from the Assyrian army by sending an angel at night to kill all their soldiers; see 2 Kings 19 verse 35, Isaiah 37 verse 36, and Hosea chapter 1 verse 7, which also alludes to this miraculous deliverance. Over a century later, however, the Babylonian monarch Nebuchadnezzar repeated the fulfilment of this prophecy against Judah when he attacked and captured their capital city, Jerusalem, and burned it down, 2 Kings 25 and Jeremiah chapters 39 and 52. God's prophecies have always been fulfilled to the letter. Let us take warning, and put our trust in Him alone for salvation!

CHAPTER 9

The LORD through Hosea reiterates Israel's guilt and their punishment in the Assyrian Exile

Although this chapter appears to repeat much that Hosea has said before, we should remember that the LORD's faithful prophet probably did repeat himself many times during the course of his long ministry, and these chapters in his book represent several originally separate sermons which he preached to the people of Israel over many years. Sadly, his people failed to respond positively to them, and the LORD's judgement fell upon them in the Assyrian invasion and conquest of 722 BC. How many times does God have to speak to us today, before we will listen to Him, and obey His word? Our natural hearts are incurably stubborn and perverted, before the LORD in grace brings us to faith in Christ, and His Spirit regenerates, and comes to indwell, us. That is one sad lesson which we can learn from Hosea's prophecy for ourselves today. Let us, therefore, respond positively to the LORD's warnings here, for our own society is very rebellious, corrupt, and sick, and severe judgement is also coming to us, if we fail to listen to God's word!

1. Israel's sins of rebellion and immorality will be punished in the coming Assyrian Exile, verses 1-9.

Verse 1 warns Israel not to rejoice at the prospect of a bumper harvest in the way that other nations did. They attributed their prosperity to their idol gods, the Baals, and Israel was doing the same. They had played the prostitute against the LORD their God, and, in worshipping their false gods, had engaged in immoral acts of love for reward on every threshing-floor. Consequently, the LORD through Hosea declares that He would invoke the covenant curses of Deuteronomy chapter 28 upon them, so that their threshing-floors and winepresses would fail to produce enough harvest to feed them. Also, in accordance with these curses, they would no longer be allowed to occupy their Promised Land, which was really the LORD's land to give or to withhold from them, but rather, they would return to a land of bondage like Egypt before their Exodus, and eat unclean food in Assyria. Here 'Egypt', as in chapter 8 verse 13, may be used figuratively for a place of bondage, rather than strictly literally, although it may be used literally in verse 6. Perhaps some Israelites, after the conquest of the Northern Kingdom by Assyria in 722 BC, escaped exile in Assyria by fleeing to Egypt, just as later in 586 BC some citizens of Judah escaped exile in Babylon by going to Egypt. In both cases, the result was disastrous. When the LORD's people were in exile, they would no longer be able to offer acceptable sacrifices and drink offerings to their covenant LORD God. In fact, their sacrifices would be unclean, like mourners' bread, as if they had touched a dead body. Such bread could only be used to satisfy their appetites, and would not be allowed to enter the LORD's temple. They would be unable to celebrate their feast days appointed for them by the LORD.

If verse 6 is referring to Egypt literally, rather than figuratively, then it is saying that destruction would sweep over them in that land, although they had escaped exile in Assyria. When they were in Egypt, they would be killed and buried in Memphis, a principal city there and famous as a burial ground. The pleasant places for their silver mentioned here may refer to their desirable houses in which they kept their silver back in Israel, or perhaps in Egypt, where they had fled. Either way, their tents, or homes, would become ruined and overrun by nettles and thorns. They would pay a heavy price for their apostasy.

Verse 7 says that the days for their punishment had now come, and Israel would certainly realise this. The meaning of the middle part of verse 7 is somewhat unclear. The Israelites may have been saying that the LORD's true prophets were fools and insane to predict as they were doing. Alternatively, Hosea may here be denouncing the false prophets of Baal for deceiving the people. Again, the last part of the verse is also difficult to understand. The AV/KJV translates thus: 'for the multitude of thine iniquity, and the great hatred'. The *James Fausset Brown* commentary offers a possible solution here, when it says that the last part of the verse may be more connected with the first part of the verse, rather than the middle part, which may be a parenthesis. The meaning would then be that the days of Israel's punishment had come because of the multitude (or greatness) of their iniquity and their intense hatred of the LORD's true prophets and every kind of spiritual good.

Verse 8 is not easy to understand clearly either. The ESV translation helps here, when it translates as follows: 'The prophet is the watchman of Ephraim with my God; yet a fowler's snare is on all his ways, and hatred in the house of his God'. The LORD's true servants never have been popular with their people, and have been the target of their hostility; only a minority of their hearers have ever believed them and responded in faith and obedience to their messages from God.

However, verse 9 is much clearer when it states the depths of Israel's corruption in Hosea's time. It was like the wickedness enacted at Gibeah in the tribe of Benjamin according to Judges chapter 19, a horrible crime of perverted lust and murder against a poor defenceless woman. How low the LORD's professing people had sunk then, and now again in Hosea's days! However, we should reflect on the perverted depravity being enacted daily in our own society today, and being partly legalised also. Here the LORD through Hosea declares that He will remember such iniquity as this, take action against its perpetrators, and punish their sins appropriately in the coming Assyrian exile. Let our unbelieving generation today take note, accept the warning, and repent before God's deserved judgement falls on them also in a similar way!

2. *Israel's idolatry and ritual prostitution will be punished by the coming exile and dispersion among the Gentile nations, verses 10-17.*
Verse 10 begins with the LORD saying what delight He had found in Israel at first, when they were in the wilderness, newly redeemed out of Egyptian bondage. They were to Him like grapes and figs which were the first-fruits in their first season. How precious to God are newly converted people, babes in Christ! Are they to us? However, such dear souls sometimes disappoint both Him and us in tragic ways. Israel certainly did, when, according to Numbers chapter 25, they fell into Balaam's trap of worshipping the Moabites' Baals at Baal-peor, and dedicated themselves to that shameful idol. By engaging in the ritual prostitution of that cult with Moabitish women, they became an abomination like the object of their adulterous love. Sadly, what Balaam had failed to achieve by attempting to curse Israel he did achieve by seduction to corrupt behaviour, and the LORD's professing people had in more recent years repeated this idolatrous behaviour many

times. Judgement must come upon them for this persistent course of apostasy.

Therefore, said the LORD, Israel's sin of involvement in the Baal fertility cult would bring upon the tribe of Ephraim, whose name means 'fruitfulness', and which was once the most numerous of the northern tribes, the covenant curses of infertility, death, and exile, so that their boasted glory would fly away like a bird. Their children would die in the imminent invasion by the Assyrians. Although the LORD saw that the tribe of Ephraim, like the coastal city of Tyre, was planted in a pleasant situation, their citizens would only beget children in order to be murdered by the Assyrians. Also, as a just punishment for their sins, the LORD would give them miscarrying wombs and barren breasts. Once the city of Gilgal in their territory had been associated with the true worship and service of the LORD, but now it was a chief centre of their idolatrous wickedness. The LORD hated them for this corruption, and had decided to drive them out of His land, which was really His house, or dwelling place. He could express His love to them no longer, because all their princes were rebellious against Him. The Northern Kingdom of Israel, represented by its principal tribe, Ephraim, would be defeated, and their roots would be dried up like a dead tree, so that they would bear no fruit. Even if they did bear children, the LORD would see to it that their beloved offspring were killed.

In verse 17, Hosea declares that his God would cast away, or reject, Israel, because they had failed to obey Him. Their punishment for wandering (or straying) from the LORD would be to become wanderers dispersed widely among all the Gentile nations in the rest of the world. The punishment would fit the crime perfectly. This was the ultimate covenant curse of Deuteronomy chapter 28 verses 64 to 68. We today know that this has become a reality until the present time. Yet we also know, from numerous other Scriptures in both Testaments, that this is not the final rejection of God's earthly people Israel, but a temporary measure of severe discipline prior to their repentance and restoration at the Second Coming of Christ to reign. Even this prophecy of Hosea supports this conclusion and prophesies Israel's restoration in several chapters both before and after this one. The LORD is both a God of infinite justice AND a God of full recovery and wonderful grace to the repentant. Failure need not be final!

CHAPTER 10

Israel's double sin of lack of fruitfulness for God and of rejecting Him as their King will be punished in the coming Assyrian Exile, unless they repent at once

As in chapters 8 and 9, in this chapter also the LORD through Hosea announces Israel's punishment for their sins, but does include a final call to them to repent. This is their last opportunity to avoid disaster.

1. Israel's unfruitfulness, hypocritical religion, and rebellion will be judged, verses 1-4.

The LORD through Hosea here states that Israel is an empty vine which only bears any fruit for itself. Many versions translate the word for 'empty' as 'luxuriant', meaning that Israel as the vine was luxuriant only in foliage, but completely barren in fruitfulness towards their God, like the barren fig tree which the Lord Jesus cursed in the Gospel records. The leaves spoke only of a formal and hypocritical profession of religion, such as the Jews exhibited during the time of Christ's earthly ministry, which was quite unacceptable to God. In Hosea's days, Israel had increased the number of the altars on which they offered sacrifices to the LORD, but, at the same time, they had improved the quality of their idolatrous sacred pillars. The LORD's people were practising a form of syncretism, a compromised religion which was quite abhorrent to Him. The truth was that their devotion and loyalty was divided between the LORD and the idols of Baal, as it was in Elijah's day during the reign of Ahab and Jezebel; see 1 Kings 18 verse 21. Therefore, the LORD found them guilty of hypocrisy, and declared that He would break down their altars and ruin their sacred pillars. Now, as a result of the imminent Assyrian invasion, which would destroy their monarchy, they would say that they had no king at all, because they had failed to fear and obey the LORD. In fact, their situation would become so desperate that they would realise that even a king could not save them from their plight under the Assyrians. In verse 4, the LORD reminds them that they had failed to be faithful to their original covenant oath, which they had sworn in Exodus chapter 19 verse 8, when they had promised to obey all the commandments that He had then just given them. Perhaps this accusation also includes the fact that the citizens of Israel had failed to keep their covenants and other agreements which they had made with one another and with neighbouring kingdoms. They had proved themselves entirely untrustworthy. This comprehensive failure in trustworthiness was the reason why judgement was now overtaking them like deadly poisonous hemlock in the furrows of a ploughed field. Once again, Hosea uses an agricultural metaphor very effectively.

2. Israel's idolatrous gods would fail to prevent the invading Assyrians from destroying their monarchy and terrorising their citizens, verses 5-8.

The LORD predicted that the citizens of Samaria, Israel's capital city, would be seized with fear, because of what they would see happening to their idolatrous golden calf image, which Jeroboam the son of Nebat had set up in Bethel. Hosea here, as elsewhere in his prophecy, names Bethel 'Beth-aven', meaning 'house of vanity (or iniquity)', because of what Israel practised there instead of worshipping God in His appointed way at the temple in Jerusalem. The people would mourn over this calf-image, and the idolatrous priests, whom Jeroboam and his successors had wrongly appointed, would shriek for it, because the Assyrians had carried it away to their own land; its false boasted glory would be lost to them. In fact, the Assyrians would take it away as a present for their king, whom Hosea again calls King Jareb, or 'King Contention'. This is probably a nickname for the invading monarch, see chapter 5 verse 13 for the other use of this name for the Assyrian king. Thus proud Ephraim would be put to shame for relying on the help of their idolatrous image, and Israel would be disappointed at the disastrous outcome of their misguided policy of making an alliance with the kings of Assyria for protection. Also, the Israelite king in Samaria would be removed by the invading Assyrians, as easily as bubbles of foam are swept away on the surface of water, or as a twig is carried away by a river. Even the high places, where Israel had committed their sin of idolatry and iniquity, would be destroyed by the invaders, so that thorns and thistles would grow up over their altars there. When Israel originally entered the Promised Land, the LORD had told them to destroy these idolatrous worship centres, but they had failed to do so. So He was going to use the invading foreign army of the Assyrians to accomplish what they had disobediently failed to do. The Israelites would become so terrified by the invasion that they would cry out to the mountains and hills to cover them, and to fall on them. They would want to die, rather than face the LORD's judgement. This verse foreshadows the reaction of unbelievers to the judgements of the coming Tribulation, which will also be the expression of God's wrath; see Luke 23 verse 30 and Revelation 6 verse 16. In reality, there neither is, nor will be, any escape from God's righteous judgement apart from confession of sin and repentance.

3. Israel will not escape suffering the disciplinary consequences of their deep and persistent sins, verses 9-11.

The LORD through Hosea again reminds Israel of the most serious sins of the men of Benjamin at Gibeah in the days of the Judges, and of their disastrous consequences in the war conducted by the other tribes of Israel against the tribe of Benjamin to avenge these; see Judges 19-20, which forms one of the most sordid stories of rape and murder in the

Scriptures. He affirms that ever since that time Israel had continued to commit sins of this nature and seriousness. Then the other tribes had stood firmly against their sinning brothers, and had not been finally overcome in their battles against the Benjamites, although the war had been won at a terrible cost in terms of lives lost. Hosea wanted his people to realise that, although the LORD had spared Israel then, He would not do so now. Israel was now not on God's side, but stood against God, and therefore would be punished, as the Benjamites had been then.

In verse 10, the LORD continues the thought by asserting, 'When it is My desire, I will chastise them, and the surrounding Gentile peoples will be gathered against them, when they are harnessed to suffer the results of their double sin of rejecting Me both as their God and as their king'. The AV/KJV translation of verse 10 is made somewhat clearer in more recent translations, but the meaning of some parts of the Hebrew for it is still rather unclear. The 'two furrows' of the older version probably refer to Israel's sins. Verse 11 is also somewhat unclear, although the general sense is that the LORD would compel Israel, whom He likens to a heifer, or cow, to engage in the difficult work of ploughing, rather than in the much easier task of threshing, as a measure of discipline for their sins. Ephraim was like a trained heifer that loved to thresh, because it was comparatively easy and allowed her to eat as she pulled the threshing sledge over the corn. Instead of this easy task, the LORD would put another yoke on her neck, and force her to pull a heavy plough. Judah also would plough. Here again Hosea includes the Southern Kingdom of Judah within the scope of his prophecy, because they were also showing signs of departing from the LORD. Then 'Jacob' here refers to the Northern Kingdom of Israel. They would certainly be compelled to break up the clods of earth in ploughing. After all their sinful waywardness, the LORD would bring both kingdoms of His chosen earthly people to heel by means of His disciplinary dealings with them. Their severe chastisement was imminent.

4. Israel will reap exactly what they have sown, whether mercy upon their thorough repentance, or disaster in the impending Assyrian invasion, verses 12-15.

It is an inevitable moral law of God's government that all men only reap exactly what they have first sown, whether blessing and eternal life for right living, or corruption and disaster for evil living. Israel was no exception to this rule, despite their blessings as God's chosen earthly nation, and neither are we today; see Galatians 6 verses 7 and 8. In verse 12, therefore, the LORD through Hosea sends to His people Israel a last fervent appeal for repentance before His judgement would fall upon them. Let them begin to live righteously, because then they would reap the abundant blessings of His mercy, His covenant love, which they had once enjoyed. They needed first to break up the untilled fallow ground of their stubborn hearts in true repentance. It was time, and there was still opportunity for them to do this, to seek the LORD in humble prayer, until He came to them in blessing, and rained the results of His imputed righteousness upon them like abundant refreshing showers.

However, in verse 13, the LORD sadly says that Israel, far from repenting, had only ploughed to produce wickedness in their lives. As a result, they were reaping a harvest of iniquity, and experiencing the bitter fruit of lying deceptions, such as their idolatrous worship and the general lack of truthfulness in the conduct of their kingdom's affairs. Instead of trusting only in the LORD their God, they had trusted in their own misguided way of worship and conduct, and had put their faith for the defence of their kingdom in the great size of their army of mighty warriors. Therefore, in verse 13, the LORD predicts that their fortified cities and castles would fail to withstand the attack of the invading Assyrian army, and there would be a great confused tumult among their citizens, such as had occurred when an Assyrian king called Shalman had plundered a city called Beth Arbel in a famous battle, and had cruelly massacred its mothers and their children. The identities of both Shalman and the city called Beth Arbel are somewhat uncertain. Shalman is probably an abbreviation for Shalmaneser, but it is uncertain which of the Assyrian kings so-named is being referred to. Beth Arbel has been identified with either Arbel, that is, modern Irbid in Jordan south-east of the Sea of Galilee, or modern Arbel two miles south-west of the Sea of Galilee. There is no other record of such a battle either in other Scriptures or in secular historical sources, but it had evidently been vividly remembered for its gross atrocities. Israel was going to be treated by the Assyrian invaders in a similar way. Verse 15 should probably be translated thus: 'So shall it be done unto you, O Bethel, because of your great wickedness'. Bethel here evidently represents the Northern Kingdom of Israel as a whole, since the symbol of their idolatrous wickedness, the golden calf-image, in which they had trusted, had been located at Bethel since the days of Jeroboam the son of Nebat. Finally, said the LORD, the king of Israel would be removed very easily in a brief morning by the Assyrians. Such would be the heavy price they would have to pay for their sins. Reader, be warned! What are we sowing today?

CHAPTER 11

The LORD expresses His caring love for Israel, mourns their ingratitude and unfaithfulness, and reluctantly confirms that He will punish them with exile in Assyria, but not destroy them completely, and await their repentance and restoration

Here the LORD through Hosea sounds a cautious note of hope for Israel's eventual repentance and ultimate restoration after their severe discipline in the coming exile.

1. *Israel would be punished with exile in Assyria for their sinful and ungrateful response to the LORD's love and care, verses 1-7.*

The LORD now expresses His true paternal love for His erring people Israel ever since He redeemed them from Egypt in the early days of their nationhood. The last part of verse 1 is quoted by Matthew in his Gospel and applied to the Lord Jesus when He was in Egypt as a baby; see Matthew 2 verse 15. Israel and the Lord Jesus were alike in that both were the objects of the love of God the Father, both were called 'My son', and both were in Egypt. In fact, Christ is the True Israel, who perfectly fulfilled for God what Israel so sadly failed to fulfil.

However, verse 2 recalls the sad fact that, when the LORD called Israel to repentance and obedience through numerous prophets, they would not listen to them, and apostatised from Him by worshipping the Canaanite Baals and burning incense to carved images. The more the LORD called them, the more they departed from Him. Although He had taught Israel to walk, as it were, by holding them by the arms, like a father guiding a young child, they did not recognise the fact that it was He who had saved and healed them from all their afflictions which they had suffered as a result of their waywardness.

Then, in verse 4, the LORD likened Israel to a work animal, which He had drawn along with the gentle cords of love in a humane and compassionate way. He had not ill-treated them, but had removed the yoke of servitude from them, and given them food to eat. Even during the dispensation of law the LORD often treated His people with a measure of grace. However, now they must be punished, not by being made to return into Egypt, but by being put under the jurisdiction of the king of Assyria. This was only necessary because they had refused to repent of their disobedient way of life. Therefore, the sword of the Assyrian king would slash down on Israel's cities, and destroy all their districts like a wild animal, because of His people's rebellious attitudes and practices. Just as the LORD had, in the past, given Israel food to eat, so now He was about to send swords, the swords of the Assyrians, to eat Israel. There is a play on words here in the Hebrew text between verse 4 and verse 6 which both use the verb *akal*, 'eat' or 'devour'. Sadly, the LORD says that His dear people

73

are continually prone to backsliding from Him. The second half of verse 7 is difficult to interpret, and no translation is completely satisfactory. Probably, the 'they' refers to the true prophets of the LORD, who continually called Israel to return to the worship of the Most High God, and were met with Israel's stubborn refusal to exalt their covenant LORD God. In other words, they absolutely refused to repent at the preaching of the prophets. However, some other translations are also possible. For example, ESV translates thus, 'and though they (meaning Israel) call out to the Most High, He shall not raise them up at all'. NIV is very similar to this.

2. In compassion, the LORD says that He will not completely destroy Israel, but that they will ultimately be restored and regathered to their Promised Land, verses 8-11.

Characteristically and very reassuringly, the LORD now expresses His extreme reluctance to give up His people Israel, because He really loved them dearly. The sad truth was that His chosen people's ungrateful and persistent sins had broken His tender heart of love for them, just as earlier in the book we saw that Gomer's unfaithfulness had broken Hosea's heart. Do we today always sufficiently consider how much we will grieve God our Father whenever we are tempted to stray into the paths of sin? Consequently, the gracious and merciful LORD felt that He could not completely destroy Israel, as He had destroyed Admah and Zeboiim (AV 'Zeboim'), the cities of the Jordan plain near Sodom and Gomorrah, see Genesis 19. His divine heart of love was churned up within Him, and His tender sympathies for His wayward people were stirred up. Therefore, in verse 9, the LORD tells us what He had resolved to do in this difficult situation. Israel must be punished, but He would not execute the full ferocity of His anger against His people, and He would not destroy Israel again in this way. The LORD reassured them that, since He is God and not man, He would not act vindictively or vengefully, as sinful mortal men do, but act with measured restraint in His disciplinary judgement. Because He is the Holy One, absolutely pure and sinless, dwelling in the midst of His wayward people Israel, He would not come with absolute terror into the city of Samaria to judge it, as He once had into the cities of the Jordan plain.

Verses 10 and 11 are even more reassuring, because the LORD here again predicts the ultimate restoration of Israel to Himself, and even their regathering to their Promised Land. This will be on the basis of the LORD's unconditional covenant promises to the patriarchs, rather than because of any merit in Israel. In that still future day of restoration, which is described in more detail in some of the other prophetical books, such as Zechariah chapters 12-14, Israel will again follow the LORD, and, in response, He will regather His people to their Promised Land from all the countries of the world where He has scattered them to this day. Hosea here likens the LORD to a lion, who will roar loudly, not then in judgement, but in order to summon His people to return from their exiles. They, on their part, will come, at last with a belated healthy respect for their LORD God, trembling in reverential fear like a frightened bird or dove, from the west, from Egypt, and from Assyria. Then He will make them dwell securely in their homes in the Promised Land again. Yes, in spite of everything that Israel has done wrong, because they are the LORD's chosen earthly people, their long-term future is secure and glorious, but by divine grace alone, as is ours as believers today! Hallelujah!

3. Returning to the current situation, the LORD begins to conclude His case against Israel, verse 12.

In the Hebrew Bible, this last verse of chapter 11 is actually the first verse of chapter 12. This chapter division is much preferable to that of the English versions, because verse 12 does begin another section of the book quite abruptly. These abrupt changes from blessing to judgement, and judgement to blessing or salvation, do characterise the book as a whole, as indeed they characterise many of the other Old Testament prophetical books. The final such abrupt change occurs at the beginning of chapter 14.

Verse 12 is a sad and sudden contrast with the verses which have just preceded it. Here Hosea returns to his theme of Israel's tragic apostasy from the LORD. The first half of the verse is quite clear in its meaning. Ephraim and Israel had dealt deceitfully and unfaithfully with the LORD. Their profession of worshipping Him with formal ritual and, at the same time, worshipping the false Canaanite idols, was completely hypocritical and unacceptable to Him. Also, Israel had been unfaithful to the LORD in forming illicit foreign alliances with the surrounding Gentile nations, and this had led them into further corruption.

However, the second half of the verse concerning Judah is rather unclear in its meaning. Translators and commentators have not been certain whether the LORD is here commending Judah, or condemning them. The RV has the following translation in its main text: 'but Judah yet ruleth with God, and is faithful with the Holy One'; but in its margin the opposite sense is given, thus: 'and Judah is yet unsteadfast with God, and with the Holy One who is faithful'. JND is similar, having the following in his main text: 'but Judah yet walketh with God, and with the holy things of truth', but in his margin he puts the opposite sense, thus: 'and Judah is yet unsteadfast as regards God and the true Holy One'. The NIV has the following: 'and Judah is unruly with God, even against the faithful Holy One'. The NASB is very similar to this. Perhaps, in the close context of chapter 12 verse 2, where the LORD says that He has a controversy against Judah also, the unfavourable interpretation of the verse is preferable. It is true that Judah still had the Davidic monarchy, which, under some of its better kings, was ruling with divine approval, and was generally more faithful to the LORD, but, in Hosea's day, they were being affected by the same corruption as the Northern Kingdom of Israel, especially under their wicked king Ahaz. So Judah was then not without fault either.

CHAPTER 12

The LORD again remonstrates with Israel, and Judah also, for their sins, which have provoked Him to anger, appeals to them to repent, and reminds them of the history of their ancestor Jacob, whom also God had to discipline

Chapter 12 verse 1 follows on directly from chapter 11 verse 12. The chapter division here is unhelpful, since it may tend to obscure the true meaning of the reference to Judah in the latter half of chapter 11 verse 12.

1. The LORD rebukes Israel for their foolish idolatry and illicit foreign alliances, verse 1.

Here, just as many times elsewhere in Hosea, the LORD addresses the Northern Kingdom of Israel by the name of Ephraim, because this tribe was its most populous and important member, and because the tribe of Ephraim had been most forward in promoting the nation's idolatry, both in the golden calf images at Bethel and Dan, and in the adoption of Canaanite Baal worship. He accuses them of feeding on wind, because they had sought to sustain their lives by worshipping futile and lifeless idols. Also, the LORD said that they had been pursuing the east wind, which in the natural world was a fierce and dangerous sirocco wind. By this He probably meant that they had been making foreign alliances with Gentile nations around them, who would only bring them into trouble and bondage. The Israelite kings had formed illicit alliances with both Assyria and Egypt at various times in order to gain the protection of these larger and more powerful nations, but the alliances had effectively backfired on them and led them into more serious military and moral trouble, not deliverance at all. Israel had ceased to trust the LORD their true God. Having dealt falsely with the LORD, they had then dealt falsely with men. They had first made a treaty with Shalmaneser, the king of Assyria; then, since they found the tribute due to him too great, they had turned to Egypt for help, seeking to win their favour by giving them the prized olive oil of their Promised Land. Eventually, the king of Egypt would fail to come to their assistance, and the king of Assyria would take vengeance upon them by invading the country and taking its citizens into exile. They would learn the cost of disobedience by bitter experience and complete ruin.

2. *The LORD declares that He also has a charge of unfaithfulness against Judah, and will proceed to punish them in a similar way to that in which He had originally disciplined their ancestor Jacob for his dishonesty and self-will, verses 2-6.*

Here the LORD says that the Southern Kingdom of Judah was no different from their brothers in the Northern Kingdom of Israel, and that He had a charge to make against them also. King Ahaz had led the nation into idolatry and political compromise with the Assyrians during Hosea's own times. This clear statement of Judah's guilt probably throws light on the meaning of chapter 11 verse 12b, which is otherwise unclear. When Hosea predicts that the LORD would 'punish Jacob according to his ways', he is identifying Judah, and probably his brothers in Israel, with their common ancestor, the patriarch Jacob, for they both had the same evil nature as Jacob had possessed which needed to be disciplined.

In verses 3 and 4, Hosea proceeds to explain the ways in which Jacob had shown his deceitful and selfish nature, even with God Himself, and relates the scene at Peniel in Genesis chapter 32, where Jacob struggled with an appearance of the pre-incarnate Christ, until God broke his natural strength and changed him. Jacob's birth had given a hint of the kind of person he would become. When he grasped the heel of Esau, his twin brother, he foreshadowed his double deception of Esau in stealing both his birthright and his blessing. Jacob had always valued spiritual things, but had sought to obtain them by wrong methods and without trusting God to see that he obtained them. He was dishonest and self-willed until his encounter with God at Peniel. There he even appeared at first to win the wrestling match with the Angelic Man, and, after God had lamed him, he clung to Him in desperate dependence with tears until God blessed him with a new name, Israel. Now, his descendants, Israel and Judah, needed to learn the lessons recorded in Genesis concerning Jacob's spiritual wrestlings with God. Like Jacob, they must both come to an end of themselves, and find their strength in the LORD alone. The LORD had found Jacob at Bethel, unexpected by him, running away from home because he had deceived Isaac and cheated Esau. There He had spoken with the ancestor of the whole nation of Israel, promising to be with Jacob until He had given him the whole Promised Land, according to His unconditional covenant with his grandfather Abraham.

In verses 5 and 6, Hosea reminds his hearers and readers that it had been the LORD God of hosts who had spoken to Jacob and all his descendants, their covenant-keeping LORD God, who had all the armies of heaven and earth at His command to bring to the aid of His people Israel. They did not need the help of Assyria or Egypt; they only needed to trust Him. Therefore, let Israel remember this, and turn in repentance to their true God. Let them keep faithful to their covenant LORD, practise merciful and loving ways with their neighbours, and also observe strict justice. They needed only to wait in true faith upon their God continually for help, rather than turn aside to other nations, and they would experience the LORD's promised covenant blessings again.

3. *The LORD exposes Ephraim's unrepentant dishonesty and idolatry, and announces that He will chastise him for this, verses 7-11.*

Verse 7 is a forthright condemnation of Ephraim, that is, Israel, for dishonesty in business transactions. The LORD through

Hosea calls him a merchant, or a Canaanite, with deceitful scales. There is a play on words here in the Hebrew text. The word for 'merchant', *Kena'an,* can also mean 'a Canaanite', a former inhabitant of the Promised Land. Canaanites were notorious for their dishonesty, but the LORD's own people Israel were just like them. How sad! They took delight in oppressing their poor customers through their extortionate business practices. Yet it was still sadder that Israel refused to recognise their sin at all, and even boasted that, since their dishonesty had enabled them to become rich, the end somehow justified the crooked means by which they had acquired their wealth. However, the end never justifies the means; both must be completely honest and honourable.

Consequently, the LORD announced their just punishment for this behaviour. He reminded them that He alone had been their covenant LORD God since the time when He had redeemed them from Egypt at the Exodus. He would make them live in tents again, as they had done in the wilderness wanderings, and as they were meant to do during the annual Feast of Tabernacles. This implies that they would be driven out of their homes and cities for their sins against Him. He also said that He had spoken to His wayward people by means of the Old Testament prophets, to whom He had given many visions and symbolical messages to deliver to Israel, in order to plead with them to repent of their sins, but this was apparently all to no avail. His people had continued in their sins of idolatry and moral corruption, as if they had never heard Him. The LORD referred to the widespread, but futile, idolatrous worship which was then being practised in Gilead, that is, in the territory to the east of the Jordan, which was actually a once-renowned Levitical city of refuge. Then He referred to the idolatrous Israelites who were sacrificing bullocks in Gilgal, to the west of the Jordan, which had originally been the place where the second generation of Israelites, who had just come out of the wilderness, had been circumcised prior to conquering the Promised Land under Joshua's leadership. Sadly, in Hosea's day there were as many idolatrous altars in Gilgal as there were heaps of stones alongside the furrows of their fields.

How quickly things can change for the worse when a nation forgets their true God! We should reflect on the sad fact that this has been happening to formerly quite Bible-believing nations in the Western World since about the middle of last century. Solemnly, we see here in Hosea what the end of such nations is likely to be in the not too distant future! Reader, again, be warned!

4. *The LORD through Hosea reminds Israel how He had disciplined their ancestor Jacob for his sins as a fugitive in Padan-aram, and how He had delivered Israel out of Egyptian bondage by means of the prophet Moses, and then He reaffirms that He will punish Ephraim for his provocative sins of bloodguilt, verses 12-14.*

The LORD now reverts to the instructive parallel which He had drawn earlier in the chapter between the experiences of Israel's ancestor Jacob and those of his descendants. Let the proud, unrepentant, sinning nation remember that Jacob had once become a fugitive for his sins against Esau and Isaac in the fields of Padan-aram, and had had to serve as a lowly shepherd for fourteen years, in order to win the hand of his favourite wife Rachel. God had disciplined him by putting him under the supervision of his uncle Laban, who was a worse swindler than Jacob had ever been. The deceiver had been deceived there in his turn, reaping exactly what he had sown. Jacob had spent twenty hard years there, before he could escape to return to Bethel again, the Lord's Promised Land.

However, as M.F. Unger points out, there is also in verses 12 and 13, a note of hope and restoration after discipline, for Jacob did eventually win his beloved Rachel as his wife, and he did return to his native country with his wives and children. Also, in verse 13, Hosea reminds his erring people that Israel had been delivered from their bondage in Egypt, after four hundred years, by the instrumentality of the prophet Moses, who was thus, under the LORD's hand, the preserver and saviour of the nation. Therefore, let Israel be assured that, although they would soon suffer conquest and exile at the hands of the Assyrians, one day they would be restored to Him and to their land. Of course, in the Northern Kingdom's case, this will need to wait until the beginning of the Millennial Kingdom of Christ, whereas Judah would be restored to their land after just seventy years' exile in Babylon. However, the main point is that the nation of Israel was going to be preserved, despite suffering heavily for their sins against the LORD.

Verse 14 returns to consider the situation in Hosea's day. Ephraim, that is, the Northern Kingdom of Israel, had provoked the LORD most bitterly to anger with their persistent sins of idolatry and consequent moral corruption. The phrase used here of Israel, 'provoked Him (the LORD) to anger', is often used in the Old Testament in connection with the sins of idolatry especially. Therefore, the LORD reaffirmed that He would not forgive the nation's bloodguilt; He would punish them severely for shedding innocent blood. He would repay them for so flagrantly dishonouring His Name. The name used here for the LORD, namely, *Adonai,* is the name of God which emphasises His sovereignty and lordship over His people. He would use His sovereign power to punish them in the coming Assyrian exile. We today worship and serve the same almighty and sovereign Lord. Let us, therefore, fear to offend Him in any way, since the consequences can be quite devastating!

CHAPTER 13

The LORD through Hosea confirms Israel's imminent punishment for their apostasy by means of the destruction of their kingdom and the slaughter of their citizens

This is the last chapter in the prophecy to reiterate Israel's sins and to announce the collapse of their kingdom. The LORD pleads with His wayward people as their only true God who has cared for them throughout their history, but sadly confirms the sentence against them. Only verse 14 possibly introduces a note of hope and reassurance, but the translation here is disputed, and may only confirm the general tenor of the chapter, which is one of doom and catastrophe.

1. Ephraim's past glory and pre-eminence will vanish away into nothing because of their national idolatry, verses 1-3.

Hosea recalls the past glory of the tribe of Ephraim in the Northern Kingdom of Israel. Probably, verse 1 should be translated, with the ESV, 'When Ephraim spoke, there was trembling; he was exalted in Israel, but he incurred guilt through Baal and died'. When Israel engaged in Baal worship from the time of Ahab and Jezebel, they lost all their respect, and suffered both spiritual death and political decline. How easy it is for us, too, to lose our good testimony before our fellowmen by the wrong actions we perform! In Hosea's day, Israel had become completely apostate, and were busy manufacturing molten images of silver, which they worshipped more and more fervently. They sacrificed to the golden bull-calf idols, which had been made by their own craftsmen, and senselessly kissed the works of their own hands. This was the lamentable extent of their wisdom and understanding.

These idols may not have been the original calf-images made by Jeroboam the son of Nebat, in order to divert the Israelites from going to worship the LORD at Jerusalem, but, worse still, images of Baal and Ashtoreth, completely pagan gods. J.M. Flanigan refers readers to 1 Kings 19 verse 18, where the LORD speaks reassuringly to Elijah concerning a faithful remnant within Israel, seven thousand altogether, of whom He says, '... all the knees which have not bowed unto Baal, and every mouth which hath not kissed him'. Perhaps the spiritual scene in Israel had grown even darker since Elijah's day in the previous, ninth, century BC, so that retribution could no longer be delayed or averted. The last part of verse 2 may read literally, '...sacrificers of men kiss calves'. This may, therefore, refer to the repulsive practice of human, or child, sacrifice, which accompanied the worship of Molech, and was allied with Baal worship.

Therefore, the LORD through Hosea announced that Israel's idolatrous kingdom could not continue any longer, and would soon pass away like a morning cloud dispersing in the sunlight, or like early dew, the chaff on the threshing floor, and the smoke from a chimney. There would soon be nothing of Israel's Northern Kingdom left in the wake of the impending Assyrian invasion. It would simply disappear from the map.

2. *The LORD reminds Israel that He had been their only Saviour God since the Exodus, and had cared for them consistently, but that they had in their pride forgotten Him, so that He must now destroy them, although He could have helped them, verses 4-13.*

In verse 4, the LORD reminds His people of His unique covenant relationship with them ever since the days of their Exodus from bondage in Egypt. He had stipulated at Sinai, in the first commandment of the Mosaic covenant in Exodus chapter 20 verses 2 and 3, that they were to worship no other gods besides Himself, since they had known no saviour besides Himself. He was pointing out the sad truth that Israel had put its trust in other nations and their own strength, rather than in His power and willingness to save them from their enemies.

In verse 5, the LORD points out to them that He had known, or rather cared for, them, all through their wilderness wanderings in a land of great drought, that is, the Sinai desert. Yet, after He had dealt with them so bountifully, so that they were fully satisfied with His provision for them, His people had shown base ingratitude towards Him. Verse 6 says that, having received plentifully from His hand, their hearts were puffed up with pride and self-sufficiency. This was why they had then forgotten their covenant LORD God. This is so frequently how materialism and affluence affect mankind. It is true of the nations of the Western world, including our own. The result of turning away from God is disastrous, both morally and spiritually, as the next verses indicate.

In verses 7 and 8, the LORD declares what He, in His absolute holiness and perfect righteousness, is about to do to Israel, His wayward sheep. He will attack them like a vicious and powerful wild animal, such as a lion, a leopard, or a bear which has been robbed of her cubs, and will devour them. He is reminding them that they were still really just as helpless as a defenceless flock of sheep, despite their pride and boasted affluence.

Then, in verses 9 to 11, the LORD, more tenderly, appeals to them in their helplessness. He points out that their present dire situation is self-inflicted, because they were against Him, who alone was their true Helper. The NASB translates verse 9 thus: 'It is your destruction, O Israel, that you are against Me, against your help', and this may be more accurate than the AV/KJV rendering. Again, the first part of verse 10 is probably more accurately translated by the NASB and the ancient versions, the Greek Septuagint, the Syriac Peshitta, and the Latin Vulgate, as, 'Where is now your king...?' The remainder of the verse is translated in a similar way to the AV/KJV rendering, and is quite clear in its meaning. The nation had clamoured for a king from Samuel, in order to be like all the nations around them, and in order that their king might save them from their enemies, forgetting that the

LORD had promised to protect and lead them. Too often the LORD's people today want to copy the ways of their unsaved neighbours in the world around them, rather than remain separate and different from them, trusting in the LORD alone. This always leads to compromise and spiritual decline. In verse 11, the LORD says that He had given them a king in His anger at their ingratitude and rebellion, but had also removed him in His righteous wrath. This had happened with the first king of Israel, Saul, who refused to obey His commandments given through Samuel. It had also happened with the dynasty of Jeroboam the son of Nebat in the Northern Kingdom of Israel more recently, and was about to happen with the last king of this division of the LORD's people, Hoshea, all for good reasons. Israel was originally intended to be a theocracy, which meant that God alone was their king ruling through delegated servants of His.

In verses 12 and 13, the LORD says that Israel's sin is bound up, or stored up like a legal document ready to be opened and dealt with in the future. Their sins are pictured as something guarded carefully until the day of retribution, when they would be opened and used as witness against the nation. The Northern Kingdom's impending judgement would come upon them like the sorrows of a woman in childbirth. Israel was like an unwise son, who refused to come out of his mother's womb at the right time of birth, despite her strenuous efforts in labour, and thus endangered the lives of both his mother and himself. The Northern Kingdom had failed to respond to the LORD's frequent calls for their repentance through His true prophets during the prolonged period of grace that He had granted them. Therefore, the LORD's judgement must finally fall upon them.

3. The LORD considers the possibility, or impossibility, of redeeming Israel from death and destruction, verse 14.

Verse 14 is a difficult verse to interpret satisfactorily in the light of its immediate context in Hosea, and also in the light of its partial quotation by the apostle Paul in his chapter on resurrection. It can be understood in one of two opposite ways, either positive and encouraging, or negative and threatening.

Many translators and commentators have understood the verse to be promising Israel deliverance by redemption from the power of Sheol and death by means of resurrection in the light of Paul's clear quotation of this verse in 1 Corinthians chapter 15 verse 55. In the latter verse, there is a note of triumphant victory over death and Hades, which is the New Testament Greek word for the Hebrew word Sheol. The AV/KJV translation in 1 Corinthians chapter 15 is indisputable, as follows: 'O death, where is thy sting? O grave (Hades), where is thy victory?' Therefore, many understand that here the LORD through Hosea is suddenly switching from His pronouncement of imminent judgement for Israel to a glorious promise of resurrection for the nation in the future; perhaps a national revival as well as a literal resurrection.

However, the last part of verse 14, 'repentance (or more probably, pity), shall be hid from Mine eyes', would then contradict the encouraging promise apparently given in the earlier parts of the verse. Hosea does indeed switch from judgement to mercy and back again several times in his prophecy, but not always quite so abruptly as this. Therefore, some translators and commentators understand the main part of the verse in a negative and threatening sense as containing two questions which require the definite answer 'No!', thus: 'Shall I ransom them from the power of Sheol? Shall I redeem them from death?'. The answer, in context, is clearly 'No!' The next two questions, which are quoted in 1 Corinthians chapter 15, would then be appeals to death to unleash its plagues and destruction against Israel, not a triumphant cry of victory over death. The last part of the verse fits this thought perfectly, since it says that the LORD will have no compassion on them. Also, the immediately following verses continue the predictions of dire judgement and death.

In 1 Corinthians chapter 15, the apostle Paul, writing by the inspiration of the Holy Spirit, is being led to adapt the verse to teach the truth of the victory of future resurrection through Christ. Sometimes elsewhere the New Testament writers do this to support their own somewhat different thoughts from those of the Old Testament writers whom they are quoting, or rather alluding to. In 1 Corinthians chapter 15 the Holy Spirit was still writing Scripture, and was free to adapt a verse from the Old Testament to support His argument concerning resurrection, even though that verse in its original context bore a very different meaning from that which He was teaching in the Corinthian letter. We should note that both J.M. Flanigan and F.A. Tatford in their commentaries on Hosea favour this negative understanding of verse 14 in its immediate context, and they may well be right.

4. The LORD's final prediction of devastating judgement on Israel and Samaria for their rebellion against Him, verses 15-16.

In verse 15, there is a play on words with the name of Ephraim, which means 'doubly fruitful', and the usual word for 'fruitful', describing Israel's contemporary prosperous condition. Jeroboam II had brought economic and material prosperity to the Northern Kingdom, but its spiritual and moral condition had been in decline. Its temporal prosperity would soon come to an end also. The LORD would soon come upon them like a hot east sirocco wind to dry up everything in its path. He is here probably alluding to the Assyrian invasion, since Assyria lay to the east of Israel, although their armies reached Israel via the Fertile Crescent, which was north of Israel. Through the instrumentality of the Assyrians the LORD would sovereignly plunder the treasure of every desirable prize in the country. Samaria would be held guilty and become desolate, because they had rebelled against the LORD their God by breaking their covenant with Him. This was the fulfilment of the covenant curses of Deuteronomy chapters 28-29. Their citizens would fall by the sword of the Assyrians, who would see that there was no future generation of Israelite children by dashing their infants to pieces, and by ripping open the wombs of their pregnant women. Such atrocities were often committed by invading armies in ancient times, and we today have heard of, or seen, similar atrocities against the victims of invasion in our own times. However, here it was the deserved judgement of God against an apostate nation, however horrific in its execution. Reader, be warned, while God still grants us a time of grace to repent!

Here we should note the fact that in the Hebrew Bible verse 16 of chapter 13 is the first verse of chapter 14, but this verse clearly continues the thought of judgement which has marked all of chapter 13, and stands in total contrast with the thought of chapter 14. The AV/KJV and all the English translations are therefore quite right to divide the two chapters after verse 16, not before it.

CHAPTER 14

The LORD's final appeal to Israel to repent, followed by His last promise of full restoration, and a final word of wisdom concerning the main lessons to be learned from Hosea's prophecy

As before in this prophecy, the LORD now changes His theme from one of severe judgement to one of salvation, hope, and restoration. As Jeremiah said in Lamentations chapter 3 verse 33, the LORD does not willingly afflict the children of men, that is, He does not take any malicious delight in causing them to suffer; His chastisement is always with a view to their repentance and restoration to fellowship again. Our sins break His heart, just as Gomer's sins broke Hosea's heart, but He really only delights to bless His people when their condition of heart and soul is right again.

1. The LORD's final appeal to Israel to repent of all their waywardness, verses 1-3.

Verse 1 is an impassioned appeal to Israel to repent and to return in heart to the LORD their only true God, recognising that they had suffered a serious catastrophe because they had so grievously sinned against Him. In verse 2, the LORD through Hosea tells His dear people what to do to get right with Him. They should decide definitely to turn back to the LORD and to fully confess their sins, then pray that He would forgive all their iniquities and, in His grace, accept them to His fellowship again. This is the same principle of confession of sins committed and full forgiveness as the apostle John teaches Christian believers today to follow in 1 John chapter 1 verse 9. Israel should then promise to praise and worship Him alone; they should never again kiss the idolatrous bull-calves as an expression of false worship, as they had done previously. The writer to the Hebrews, in chapter 13 verse 15, alludes to this verse in connection with the sacrifices of praise which Christians today should offer to God as the New Testament priesthood, thus: 'By Him therefore let us offer the sacrifice of praise to God continually, that is, the fruit of our lips, giving thanks (or confessing) to His Name'.

Verse 3 then explains what the practical results of Israel's true repentance will be in terms of a changed life, for without a clear change of behaviour there cannot have been any real repentance. Israel will say that they would no longer make illicit alliances with Assyria, in order to save their kingdom, but would rely solely on the LORD's help. Nor would they use cavalry horses in battle like the surrounding Gentile nations, in order to strengthen their military power. The LORD had forbidden Israel's kings to multiply horses for this purpose, but had instructed them to trust in Him alone for defence, see Deuteronomy 17 verse 16. Neither would they any longer treat their hand-made idols as their gods, as they had so persistently done in the past, but instead would turn to the

LORD, who alone could be a source of comfort and mercy to the poor defenceless orphans.

2. The LORD's wonderful and gracious promises to Israel of full and final restoration and prosperity in Himself and His love, verses 4-8.

Now the LORD, in a remarkable series of promises, declares how He will bless Israel after they have repented and returned in heart to Him again. Here there is no detailed prediction concerning when precisely this will happen to His earthly people, as there is in a few other parts of the Scriptures, but only the general promises are given. In fact, we know, chiefly from Zechariah chapters 12-14, that Israel will not finally repent and turn to the LORD before they see Christ coming to save them at Armageddon at His glorious Second Coming to reign. Then the blessings of this chapter will be experienced by them to the full. They were not really experienced in any full measure by the people of Judah when they returned from their seventy years of exile in Babylon, since, as Daniel chapter 9 verse 25 states, those days were 'troublous (troubled) times'. Thus we see from various Scriptures that Israel's restoration, blessing, and glory still all lie in the future, but they are certain to be fulfilled, because their promises rest on the unconditional covenants which the LORD made with the patriarchs, Abraham, Isaac, Jacob, and David. Israel's future blessing depends on God alone! Hallelujah!

Three times in two verses the LORD gives His assurance, 'I will'. Apart from that, Israel would be forever lost and separated from their covenant God. In verse 4, the LORD promises that He will heal all Israel's backsliding and its sadly wounding results, and will love them freely. His is a self-sacrificial, unconditional love for the unlovely, as we also have experienced. In the day of restoration He will turn His fierce anger away from them, for judgement is His 'strange work', as He says in Isaiah chapter 28 verse 21. In verse 5, the LORD says that He will become like refreshing dew to Israel, which will enable the nation to grow and blossom into flower like a lily of the field, beautiful and fragrant. This will be the complete opposite of what He had predicted in judgement, in chapter 13 verse 15, as a result of the Assyrian invasion. Further, in the latter part of the same verse, Israel in their prosperity is likened to a stable cedar of Lebanon with deep roots in their covenant LORD God. Tall and majestic like a cedar of Lebanon, their branches will spread out widely to give shelter to all under them, their beauty will resemble the luxuriant olive tree, and their aromatic smell will remind everyone of the fragrant Lebanon mountain region. Verse 7 is perhaps more accurately translated thus: 'Those who live in his shadow will again raise grain, and they will blossom like the vine. His renown will be like the wine of Lebanon' (NASB). Right up until Israel's repentance and restoration, the LORD's earthly people will have been a stench in His nostrils, fit only for severe discipline. However, in the Millennial Kingdom of Christ, Israel will be an honour to their covenant God, His faithful witnesses to all the other nations, and the leading nation on earth; not the least significant as they are today. What a complete transformation the LORD will accomplish then! Praise Him for the glory of His sovereign grace!

Verse 8 has been variously translated and understood, but it is best understood as a short conversation between the LORD and restored Ephraim, that is, Israel. We should probably supply the words, 'shall say' after Ephraim, as the AV does in italics, although the Hebrew original text does not include them. The meaning then is that Israel will, in the day of their repentance, say, 'What have I any more to do with idols?' For centuries God's people were plagued by idolatry, from the time that they were in Egypt right up until the Babylonian exile of Judah. Judah was cured of this sin during their exile. However, the nation will again succumb to idolatry during the Tribulation, when many of them will worship the idolatrous image of the Man of Sin, probably the first Beast of Revelation chapter 13, which he will set up in the rebuilt temple in Jerusalem, until the LORD destroys him at His appearing in glory at Armageddon. Then, and not until then, will both Israel and Judah be finally purged of the sin of idolatry, repenting of their sins with great mourning. That will be a most joyful day for the LORD their true God. He will say, in the words of the second part of verse 8, according to the NASB translation, 'It is I who answer you and look after you', that is, not your man-made idols. Israel will at last have learned this basic spiritual lesson. Then He will say that He Himself is like a green fir, or cypress, tree to Israel, the source of His restored nation's prosperity, and will assert that Israel's ability to bear fruit for Him is only to be found in Him. As J.M. Flanigan says, 'In a word, every desirable thing was in Him to whom they had been happily restored'.

3. The Epilogue, a word of wisdom on the lessons to be learned from Hosea's prophecy, verse 9.

So we reach the final verse of Hosea's poignant prophecy, which reveals his own broken heart over his adulterous wife Gomer, and also the LORD's broken heart of love for Israel because of their persistent sins against Him; the first situation purposely illustrating the second, and even more serious, one. He has rehearsed his people's sins several times over, has repeatedly predicted their grievous punishment in the impending Assyrian exile of 722 BC, but has also promised the ultimate complete restoration of His beloved nation in a day yet future to us today, after they have repented and been purged of their paramount sin of idolatry with all its accompanying moral corruption. Thus the message of Hosea's prophecy is positive as well as negative, and it ends on a very joyful note, namely, Israel back in their Promised Land during Millennial days bringing blessing and prosperity to all the inhabitants of the world during Christ's kingdom. That was the LORD's true desire for Israel all along, and

He has a similar desire for the blessing of all His redeemed people in both Testaments, which He will ultimately realise and accomplish, in spite of everything that opposes His sovereign will.

What, then, does verse 9 say are the lessons that we should learn today from Hosea's prophecy? First, that the ways of the LORD are always right in every respect. This refers here primarily to the LORD's covenant demands upon His people Israel, which they refused to acknowledge so often. Secondly, that the righteous, that is, faithful believers in every age, live according to them, obeying them conscientiously. Thirdly, that those who transgress His commandments will stumble (AV 'fall') over (not in) them, and incur the righteous punishment for their sins. These are simple, but searching, lessons to learn, but, if we, like Israel, fail to learn them by the easier way of obeying the word of God to us as soon as we hear and understand it, we will need to learn them by the much harder way of bitter experience and spiritual loss.

Hosea thus finishes his book with a solemn warning to all his readers. God is always right in whatever He does, whether we understand this or not, and the only way to receive His blessing and enjoy unbroken fellowship with Him is to trust and obey Him implicitly at all times. May we therefore live daily in the good of these basic lessons of spiritual experience, recognising that our gracious and holy LORD only desires our ultimate blessing and good, which is also, and primarily, for His own transcendent glory!

Israel's Broken-hearted Prophet